Dedication:
WHAT IT'S ALL ABOUT

Dedication:
WHAT IT'S ALL ABOUT

Marjorie A. Collins

BETHANY FELLOWSHIP, INC.
Minneapolis, Minnesota

ISBN 0-87123-103-4

Copyright © 1976
Bethany Fellowship, Inc.
All rights reserved

Published by Bethany Fellowship, Inc.
6820 Auto Club Road, Minneapolis, Minnesota 55438

Printed in the United States of America

*Dedicated to
my mom and dad and
to a multitude of friends,
supporters and counselors who,
though unnamed, have helped me along
the pathway of commitment.*

MARJORIE A. COLLINS

Miss Collins is a native of Maine. She received a B.A. in Bible and Missions from Providence-Barrington Bible College, and did work in Creative Writing at the University of Miami.

She was a missionary in Pakistan for about four years and personnel secretary with the World Radio Missionary Fellowship. She has also occupied administrative and secretarial positions in Boston, Rhode Island, and Florida.

At the present time she is a free-lance Christian writer.

Her articles have been published in over thirty periodicals, including *Moody Monthly, Christian Life, The Pentecostal Evangel* and *Eternity.*

She has, in addition, authored at least seven other books prior to *Dedication: What It's All About.*

Foreword

This book recaptures a word that has been kidnapped by false religionists and political ideologists. It doesn't merely display the corpse but breathes new life into it. Isn't it always astonishing to witness a resurrection and equally exciting when hostages are released? When a "typical high school student" can be changed into a screaming revolutionary in a few years while the church remains adament and anemic, it is unquestionably time to redefine and reevaluate dedication. We have been floundering in our own pollution too long when the secular world must show us the meaning of Christian words. This book closes the door of escape for those who would just shrug their shoulders in pious quiescence or for those who have thrown up unholy hands in consternation. The current casualty rate of young Christian devotees cannot be explained by merely blaming the day in which we live. Admittedly, many Christian organizations have long since reached the "bottom of the barrel." However, I concur with the author when she intimates that we are, possibly, looking in the wrong barrel.

Each chapter in this interestingly written book is a breath of fresh air, ventilating mustiness from a house with form but no life. The author is perceptive in dealing with traditionalism, over-simplification and devastating generalities. She is not only a good diagnostician, but her writing is solution-oriented, with a clearly presented synthesis. It is refreshing to read something that is more than symptomatic and superficial; and a positive approach to any problem is always encouraging. The author is telling us that it is not only full-time Christian service that is needed, but full-time Christians. It is not dedication to a program but to a person. It is not an appeal merely to logic or emotion, but rather to love and devotion.

Speaking from her own missionary experience, the author is most discerning of the true purpose of missions, namely, the necessity of establishing the indigenous church. Dedication to this concept is enhanced by modern methodology and techniques, bringing a new formula for missions: One committed missionary today may well equal ten of previous years. When most of the countries of the world are suffering from national nervous breakdowns, and are devoid of direction and purpose, we have an awesome responsibility to declare and personify our message.

It is always a little painful when a writer takes the veneer and cheap shine off Christian service, but helpful when the hurts are dealt with compassionately. She not only writes about, but exemplifies, the penetrating inner glow of a committed life.

As a missionary-minded pastor desiring to give leadership to a missionary-oriented church, I am faced with certain realities. There are far too many dedications and far too few disciples;

far too many spectators and far too few participants. The book is helpful with its spiritual format and with pragmatic suggestions for thirsting Christians. Occupational therapy really does wonders for most of God's people.

Finally, the book says what needs to be said regarding the church's part in dedication: to take care of those who have dedicated themselves, to show loving care, and to keep in touch by developing communication interchange. It is *walking an aisle* and obviously one must have this short view of the act of dedication, but in the overview, many people are really not dedicated, says the author—not if we define dedication in terms of scripture as a "death sentence." Death is never a token of something temporary; rather, it is characterized by permanence and absoluteness. A dear saint reminds us that a man on a cross certainly has no further plans of his own; that he is looking only one way; and that obviously he is not planning to go back home at the end of the day. Dedication is a personal relationship with Jesus Christ; a total commitment to an eternal purpose; and death to self.

Something is being done about dedication, but something more needs to be done. Strong personal involvement with strong church involvement results in strong disciples. God has been sovereignly creating a huge manpower pool of committed youth in this decade, and His Spirit is now calling them to a genuine walk with God. This book, *Dedication: What It's All About* will tell you how.

Rev. William B. Bedford, D.D.
The Village Church
Shell Point Village
Fort Myers, Florida

Preface

At a recent missionary conference, I ran into an old friend. We talked a few minutes and then he said, "My heart is filled to overflowing with the fact that at our meeting [in another city] last evening, 60 young people dedicated their lives to the Lord for full-time service."

A while back, a missionary was brought from some distance and at a goodly amount of money to be the main speaker for our missionary conference in a southern city. He was present from Friday night through Wednesday. At the close of the final service on that last day, an invitation was given for young people to respond to the commission of Christ to "Go . . . and tell." Seven young people went forward. Six had gone in previous conferences. The seventh was a slightly retarded boy of 14, who loved the Lord dearly. The next day, as we were taking the missionary speaker to his plane, he seemed very discouraged and extremely disappointed.

"Why the long face?" we questioned. (We had known him for many years and were good friends.) Then he poured out his grief over the fact that there was among the young people of our church no sign of desire to give their lives to the Lord, or to be used of Him wherever He might lead.

Years ago I heard a man testify concerning his dedication experience. He said, "When the invitation was given at the close of the service, I was the only one who responded. Later the following conversation was overheard.

"How was your service tonight, John?"

"Oh, it was pretty good. But there was no response. Only one little 7-year-old boy came forward."

Today if you were to hear the name of that one little boy, you would recognize it immediately. He went on to be one of the finest gospel singers, personal evangelists and teachers of our country. His impact has literally circled the globe through his missionary interest.

Somehow Christians measure the effectiveness of special meetings, missionary conferences and young people's rallies by the number who raise their hands and/or walk forward to "dedicate themselves" to the Lord. In some cases there is joy because there is a "good" response. At other times there is disappointment because of the seeming lack of response.

But whether the results are great or small, there is a further consideration to be taken into account. This was forcefully brought to my attention by my friend, Dr. Clarence W. Jones (Cofounder and Honorary Chairman of the Board of the World Radio Missionary Fellowship, Inc.— HCJB), who was speaking recently at a missionary conference in Boston, Massachusetts. Between sessions he sought me out and said, "Marge, someone's got to write something on a very important subject. I think it should be called 'Missionary Volunteer Follow-Through!' I've discussed this with Harry Liu (Pocket Testament League), and he wholeheartedly concurs with me. But I don't have time to commit it to paper. Why don't you see what *you* can do with it?"

Then he began to share his concerns about what happens to the young person who steps forward, or raises his hand, or makes a commitment in a service of dedication. He also suggested that, in the day in which we live, there is a real need for older folks to step out in dedication, too.

"There's a terrible gap at this point," Dr. Jones continued. "And no one seems to be doing anything about it. Suppose a baseball player stands at the plate. The ball comes flying toward him. He swings the bat and makes contact, but the moment the bat hits the ball, the player stops swinging! Or suppose a golfer tees up his ball and prepares for his shot. Back go his arms. His legs are where they should be. His elbows and wrists are in perfect position. He keeps his head down and his eye on the ball. Down comes the club, but the moment he hits the ball, he stops his swing. What is the result? Almost everything these men had hoped would happen to their ball has come to an abrupt end, for the simple reason that there was no follow-through!"

I knew exactly what he meant. I had seen it happen over and over again. I know from personal experience that from the moment I dedicated my life to the Lord for whatever He might choose for me to do, I was on my own. The work of the pastor, the church, the special speakers was accomplished. I had come to that moment in life when I desired to be wholly His. Beyond that, it was left to *my* time, *my* prayers, *my* circumstances and *my* personal investigation to get me to that day when I was presumed to be "prepared and meet for the Master's use."

Pastor, preacher, missionary, teacher, parent, friend: Are you willing to put some effort into Dedication Service Follow-Through? Are you at least interested in knowing how this can be possible?

The book you now hold in your hand has been written for that purpose. May God use it to capture and keep your love and interest focused on those who could and would turn the world upside down for Jesus Christ—if you will do your part.

Contents

Foreword

Preface

1   What's Dedication All About? 17

2   Who Is Dedication For? 26

3   What's To Be Dedicated To? 38

4   What Do Dedicated People Do? 44

5   Is Dedication Only for Foreign Service?... 53

6   After Dedication, What? 57

7   Does Dedication Last? 70

8   Is There More To Be Said About
    "Full-Time" Service? 74

9   Who Should Give an Invitation to
    Dedication? 79

10   Who's Doing Anything About
    Dedication? 88

11   Are You *Honestly* Dedicated? 96

12   Dedication, Discipleship and
    Destination 108

13   How Much Does Dedication Cost? 120

14   What Problems Does Dedication Raise? . . 131

15   The "S" Sense of Dedication 145

1

What's Dedication All About?

If you've lived for any length of time, you've probably received an invitation (or dozens of them) to attend the dedication ceremony for an infant, a building, an organization or a park. It may or may not have seemed important to you; you may or may not have attended.

In the Christian world, we are forever hearing about "dedication." We are nearly inundated with requests for dedication. Our money, our home, our children, our automobile, our talents, our abilities, our joys, our life—we are told that all must be dedicated to the Lord. Oh yes, there are plenty of good scripture verses to back it up, too.

Solomon built a house to the name of the Lord his God and dedicated it to Him (2 Chron. 2:4). He used furnishings in it that David had dedicated to the Lord (2 Chron. 5:1). God asks His people to sanctify themselves and be holy (Lev. 20:7), i.e., dedicate themselves to Him. The Lord even suggested that the people dedicate their homes when He said, "What man is there that hath built a new house, and hath not dedicated it? let him go and return to his house, lest he die in battle and another man dedicate it" (Deut. 20:5).

We are told that the old covenant was dedicated with blood (Heb. 9:18) just as the new covenant was. The Jewish calendar includes a day for the Feast of Dedication to celebrate the reconsecration of the temple after its pollution by the Syrians (John 10:22).

So dedication is not a strange word to God-fearing people. And it is little wonder that the process of providing a dedication service has become the norm in many churches. It's a great idea—usually!

Unfortunately, there are the few rotten apples which try to spoil the whole basket. Perhaps you've been through such an experience, noting someone who was an egotist, or a statistician, or an organizational person, or a numbers man (or woman— let's not exclude half the people on earth), who has to attain certain goals in his meetings. He gives an invitation to salvation, dragging it on and on. Just when the congregation expects that the last convert has been wrenched from his chair and the benediction will be pronounced, a whole new invitation is given—an invitation to dedication. If you already know Christ, then you must serve Him.

"Now who will give up his right to himself and come forward to dedicate his life in service to the Lord?" No one goes forward.

"And how many will be willing to give up the comforts of their present existence and come forward to dedicate their lives in service to Christ?" Again no one moves.

We run the gamut of fleshly lusts, desires, ambitions and sins until there's nothing more to give up, even if we were willing. This wringing and squeezing will usually produce some kind of response—if only to get the service over with so folks can go home and get the kids to bed! The figures look great. Eight accepted the Lord; six dedicated their lives to the service of Christ.

But what was the compelling force behind these actions? What meaning does the experience have in the lives of those who are now "dedicated"? What does it mean to be dedicated? Was the whole experience a pleading for numbers or was it truly the work of the Holy Spirit?

It's strange how many words we accept at face value with very little, if any, understanding of their true meaning. We all know what the word "dedication" means. Why define it?

All right, then. What *does* it mean? How would *you* explain it? Are you thinking about it? What have you decided?

Now, let's compare *your* understanding of "dedication" with the plain facts concerning it as found in the dictionary, and let's see how they compare.

We're going to peek into Webster's Third New International Dictionary (G. and C. Merriam Co., 1966) and see what we find.

"Dedication: Act or rite of dedicating to a divine being or to a sacred use." (Didn't someone teach us never to define a word by using it in the definition?) And then comes "solemn appropriation."

Now we've got more troubles. What does the word "appropriation" mean? Webster tells us it means "to appropriate to oneself or another person or to a particular use." Rather confusing, since it, too, defines itself by itself. But at least we've progressed to the point where dedication involves transferring our interests to a particular use.

Appropriation also implies "imitative behavior." (Remember that we are speaking in terms of a dedication of our lives to the service of Christ, and in particular to full-time ministry, if God should lead in that direction.) What kind of behavior are we to imitate?

It seems quite plain that we must imitate Jesus himself. Paul felt that way, for he wrote, "Be ye therefore followers of God, as dear children; and walk in love, as Christ also hath loved us, and hath given himself for us . . . " (Eph. 5:1, 2). Peter makes it even clearer when he says, "For even hereunto were ye called: because Christ also suffered for us, leaving us an example, that ye should follow his steps" (1 Pet. 2:21).

Webster's definition goes further. "Dedication," says he, "is a devoting, or setting aside for a particular purpose." He then explains how this works out in a given legal matter. Suppose you own an acre of ground. You hold title to that plot of ground. But because it is in an ideal location and has a great deal of potential, you turn your deed over to the city fathers along with a dutifully signed agreement stating that this parcel of earth is given in perpetuity for the purpose of a children's playground. In so doing, you not only relinquish any rights you previously held on that property, but no one else has any right to assert ownership inconsistent with the use for which the property has been dedicated.

Is there any legality to the matter of volunteering for full-time Christian service? Oh, you say, we live under grace—not under law. But is it not possible to conceive that the law of love is far more strict than the legality of law? The dedication service should not be something that is entered into with no thought or little consideration. It involves responsibilities. It involves cutting the ties of ownership. The individual gives up his little acre of land. It was purchased at tremendous cost. Paul says, "For ye are bought with a price: therefore glorify God in your body, and in your spirit, which are God's" (1 Cor. 6:20). And in the next chapter he adds, "He that is called, being free, is Christ's servant. Ye are bought with a price; be not ye the servants of men" (1 Cor. 7:22, 23). So we don't give God something for nothing in our act of dedication. He's paid far more for it than it's worth! But the main point is that He has, in fact, purchased us.

Now we are saying that at the act of dedication, we are giving up all right to ourselves from that point forward. And we are also obligating our heirs to our commitment.

The wonderful part is that when we give our lives to God in dedication, we have the privilege of choosing the use to which our lives will be dedicated. And since God is merciful and kind, He doesn't even hold us to that original purpose we might have had in mind. This is where love enters beyond the law. You see, our acre of ground can never be used for anything but a children's playground, even if someone later decides it would serve more people better as a parking lot. Those are the terms on which the land was offered. Usually a dollar is offered in payment, to clinch the transaction. The signature on the agreement confirms the terms. They can never be changed by you, your descendants, or the city fathers.

God, on the other hand, is much more loving and lenient. And He is far wiser than we. We may dedicate ourselves for a particular purpose. He may lead us in an entirely different direction. But the main thing is, the contract has been signed and the deed is in His hand. It is legally binding, and if we fail to keep our end of the commitment, we must expect the fullest expression of God's blessing to depart from us. Why? Because we are asserting our right of ownership to that which is no longer ours. This can produce nothing but chaos.

So dedication is a solemn appropriation of ourselves to God. It is a legal transaction which ought to be binding upon us. God keeps His part of the bargain; never doubt that. But what about you?

Another facet of truth in the act of dedication comes in an entirely different realm. "Dedication," says Webster, "can be used as a prefix to literary, musical or artistic production, expressing admiration or affection for a person or for a cause."

This book has a dedication page. Most books do. Look at some of your choir music. Many pieces are dedicated to churches, choirs or individuals. It is an honor to the one to whom these things are dedicated. It shows a true bond of loving, appreciative friendship and gratitude. And in dedication, we show our love and gratitude to our God for His care of us—past, present and future. It shows our confidence in Him. It tells others where our allegiance lies. Better than that, though, is the fact that it brings honor and glory to God, which, as we have seen (1 Cor. 6:20) is the norm for those who have been purchased by Him at great cost.

Webster's final definition of dedication is well worth considering. He explains it as a "self-sacrificing devotion to a cause: zeal, faithfulness, enthusiasm." Again, we look at the word "devotion" and find it means "setting apart and providing for use; giving up (time, money, thought, effort) to the cause, for the benefit, or to the advancement of something regarded as deserving support, improvement or aid; attaching your attention and activities on a specified object, field or objective."

Too often dedication has been a time for "setting apart" but not followed by "providing for use." Too often dedication has been followed by "giving up" without remembering that the definition tells us what to give up and why it's necessary to do so. And too often dedication has meant "attaching yourself" to that which the church practically requires of its young people (i.e., going forward in a dedication service) with no specified object, field or objective in mind.

How does *your* definition of dedication compare now with what we've gathered together? Does it include any or some or all of these elements?

1. Giving yourself over to God for His own use.

2. Transferring your interests to the service of Christ.

3. Imitating the Lord Jesus in your daily walk and talk.

4. Turning over to God your rights to yourself.

5. Expressing your admiration and affection to

God, thus bringing honor and glory to Him.

    6. Self-sacrificing devotion to God pursued with zeal, enthusiasm and faithfulness.

    7. Being set apart to God and a willingness to be used by Him.

    8. Giving up those things which would hinder in your ministry for Him.

    9. Attaching your attention and activities on the will of God for your life.

    10. Choosing an objective (a goal) for your life in terms of your devotion to Him.

Abraham Lincoln was a man of dedication. Read his life. Read his speeches. He knew where it was at. True, he was dedicated to a cause which was not specifically related to the church and its teachings. But if dedication can be defined by the life of an American, Lincoln is our man. What he said at Gettysburg concerning those who had laid down their lives in battle must be said of those of us who are called the soldiers of Christ, namely, "It is . . . for us to be here dedicated to the great task remaining before us" (Address, Gettysburg, November 19, 1863). And what a great task we have! The evangelization of the world! (Acts 1:8) And then the perfecting of the saints, the work of the ministry, and the edifying of the body of Christ (Eph. 4:12).

Dedicating one's life for Christian service is not simply a stepping out, a walking forward, a prayer, a hand shake and dismissal. It is a legal, binding, current contract with God. It must not be entered into lightly as so many contracts are today. It must come only after being thoroughly explained so that those who respond know full well the implications of what they are doing. It must be a meaningful and logical step in commitment to God and His will. If it is a mere statistic, a step intended to get dad or mother, husband or wife, teacher or pastor "off your back" forget it!

Dedication must come of a free mind and a willing spirit if it is to come to fruition. It should be a source of strengthening and obedience. It ought to be a time of seeking, searching and settling.

Of course, dedication may not be a big happening. It may not come through an altar call. It may not be induced by the pleas of a preacher. It can come in the quietness and confidence of knowing that God is leading you to give your life in service for Him. It can come any time, in any place, in any way, to anyone.

The main thing, of course, is the response which is given to the call when it comes. If it is dismissed or overlooked, it may soon be forgotten. It may never come so clearly again. In fact, it may never come again.

But if you have heard His call and will gladly respond to it, its intensity and clarity will increase. And God will consecrate you to His service. Consecrate? Yes! He will "induct you into a permanent office, confirm you officially, declare you holy, set you apart and devote you to His worship and service." That's what dedication is all about!

"I am the Lord your God, which have separated you from other people" (Lev. 20:24).

2

Who Is Dedication For?

When we think of the dedication of life to Christian service, we often think in terms of young people. During a dedication invitation, we expect high school and college-aged people to respond. If youngsters go forward, we are apt to take little note of it. If older folks were to stand up and be counted, we would question their ability to fulfill their commitment.

Throughout our Christian experience, we have somehow gotten the idea that dedicating one's life to Christian work must be done between the ages of 15 and 25. At 15, of course, a young person will begin to look toward and plan for the future. He must choose a profession. He must choose a college which will prepare him in his field or specialty. He must prepare his parents for his flight from the nest. He must assure himself that this is what his heart truly desires.

But such choices must come to an end no later than age 25! If someone is to get to the mission field, for example, it is imperative that he go before age 30! This leaves him only 5 years in which to get his education, settle his affairs, raise his support and step foot on foreign soil before that formidable turning point in life is reached.

This, I repeat, is what has been hammered into our dull minds. Little wonder, then, that no emphasis is placed upon the necessity for children to look forward to Christian service. (There is no harm in their looking forward to becoming a nurse, doctor, teacher or pilot, you understand—but they're far too young to consider being a missionary, a pastor, or a Christian Education worker.) And those over the 30 mark? Sorry. Too old! They could never adjust to a new climate, culture, language, customs, food, etc. Their minds are not as keen as they once were, so learning Japanese, or Arabic, or even Spanish would be an insufferable task eliminating the possibility of the mission field. And they are also too old to begin training for the ministry at home. Then, too, they might have to give up something in the homeland, for their homes are already established. They may have older parents who need their presence in order to survive. They may have a family of their own, and how would the children ever be able to cope with being M.K's (missionary kids) or P.K's (preacher's kids)?

I dedicated my life to the Lord for missionary service when I was 14 years of age. Although I was "underage," at least I was tall, and many folks probably thought I was older! It was a very real commitment on my part. I had been saved a little over a year. Now I was in the first row of the balcony at a missionary conference in a small New England church. We were singing, "I'll go where you want me to go, dear Lord . . ." and I went all the way from the balcony to the front of the church. A man from the Philippines had spoken. I don't even remember his name. But when he stood up and asked who would be willing to dedicate his life to full-time Christian service, I was one of the first to respond. I was not coerced into this decision. As I look back, I am sure the Holy Spirit had been preparing my heart for several months, and this was an open confession of my willingness to respond.

Twenty years later, I was in another missionary conference in the South. Between the two conferences, I had completed high school and Bible college, spent two years in deputation work, four years on the mission field in West Pakistan, a year as a Christian Education Director and almost six years of work in the home office of a well-known missionary organization. At the close of the conference, an invitation was given.

"And who will respond to the challenge of missionary work? Who will come forward, and by so doing will say, 'Lord, I'm willing to be a missionary if you lead me in that direction'? "

Ten or 12 young people moved forward—all between the ages of 17 and 21. After a bit of prodding with no further visible response, the speaker said, "Now if any of you have previously committed your life to the Lord for full-time service, come and join these standing at the front."

The Lord had led me out. He had just as directly led me home. Had I put my hand to the plow and turned back? No! Had I failed in my responsibility to Him? No! Was I still willing for missionary service? Yes! But should I go forward? I pondered the question for some moments and decided not to go. The reason some of the others were there was because they had gone before, but felt urged to go forward at every invitation. About half were making a first-time decision. Then the speaker made it clearer.

"If you have ever dedicated your life to the Lord in the past and are still willing for His will in your life, please step forward." This was the way I felt, so I left my pew and stood at the front of the church—at the ripe old age of 34. The people in that church knew me. I had been a member for six years. But they looked askance at me. I was just too old to be trotting down the aisle as an indication of any type of dedication to the Lord.

My question was, am I the only one willing to be willing, or am I the only one foolish enough to let anyone know I'm willing to be willing? In either case, I thought it was a pity. Yet, I realize there are those who are not typically demonstrative (including myself), and therefore hold back, either putting off the decision, or making it "in the secret of their heart."

Is dedication open commitment or should it be a sort of secret society like the Masons or the Odd Fellows? Is it so obscure in meaning that only those who have experienced it know what it's all about? And if so, what an indictment this is against the Christian church.

We have only to look around us to see how far we have fallen short of the mark in seeking those who will be willing to serve God as a lifetime profession.

What has happened in England through the centuries? The heir-apparent to the throne, from the time of earliest childhood, has been prepared for becoming the king (or queen) of the British Empire. He is set apart. He goes to special schools, He is drilled in history, law, order and the social aspects of the position he will one day assume. He knows where he is headed, and everyone (hopefully) helps him to get where he's going.

Those in the priesthood are given over to the study of the church, the discipline of the church, the schooling of the church and the functioning of the church from childhood. They are well saturated, well trained and well prepared for the ministry they will assume.

In the land of India, there is no longer a legal caste system because of governmental mandates against it. Nevertheless a type of caste system persists. A sweeper's parents teach him to sweep as soon as he can toddle. He is practically consumed with it. There is little time for any other endeavor. The same is true of the fruit vender, the brass maker, the political man and the carriage driver.

Some cultures, philosophies and religions say, "Give me a boy until he's 12 years of age, and then you can have him back." The implication is, of course, that if a boy is educated and trained in any one particular thing for the first 12 years of his life (be it communism, Catholicism, atheism, agnosticism or any other of a thousand and one "isms"), no matter what happens after that, who tries to change his mind or teach him something different, he will be what he was taught to be. The pattern will be set. The mold will be hardened.

But what does the Protestant Christian Church do in most instances? It holds Sunday school classes and church services. In some areas it holds week-day Bible classes or Home Bible clubs. It puts up with a short vacation Bible school program. Some churches are now making provision for Christian nurseries and Christian day-schools. And what are we teaching our children? "Bible truths," you say? Hopefully this is true. But what is included in those Bible truths?

Does not the basic thrust of teaching revolve around one great theme, i.e., salvation from sin through faith in Jesus Christ? I have heard Sunday school teachers decry the fact that the material in their Beginner's curriculum did not always contain a salvation invitation. It taught that God is love, God is good, God is present, God is our heavenly Father, and God is real. We have forgotten that basic facts must be taught before a foundation has been laid sufficiently solid enough to undergird a Christian life. Of course salvation is important and imperative. But there must be more to Christian teaching than this, that Christ died on the cross to save us from our sins. Not only must we do some groundwork so that when the seed is planted it will find root and be able to germinate, but once the child has understood the claims of the gospel and his own responsibility in believing, must he continue to be bombarded with a "simple believism" message? When he has accepted the Bible as true and has come into a living, loving relationship with God through Jesus Christ, must he continue to hear the same message reiterated in almost the same way throughout his lifetime?

I'm afraid this is the very reason that we are losing so many of our young people today. They become saturated to the point of boredom with the one message, "Jesus saves." They know it. They believe it. They've experienced it. But *now* what? Or perhaps we should ask, "So what?" Do we trust the decision which has been made? Do we believe the child understood what he was doing? Do we make him feel that he may not have truly meant what he said or did—or perhaps he did it because someone else did it? Is that why we keep at him with the same emphasis week after week, month after month and year after year?

It is a pitiful thing when this happens. But what can we do about it? First of all, we need to start at the beginning. We need to teach the Word of truth in a way and on a level with the ability of the child to learn. As he progresses in his knowledge in and acceptance of the Word (both the written Word and the living Word), he should be taught more truth and deeper insights. He should build upon that which has been laid as a foundation. You don't teach calculus before teaching that $2 + 2 = 4$. Neither do you teach the basic math table when the student is ready for trigonometry. "Line upon line, precept upon precept"—that was Isaiah's wise instruction to those who would teach (Isa. 28:10). You can't build a brick wall by laying a first row of bricks twenty times. You build a wall brick upon brick, row upon row. You can't build a strong and useful Christian by laying the foundation twenty times in twenty places, or by laying the top row first. But truth must be built upon truth until the finished product is a demonstration of a building which will not collapse at the first storm which beats against it.

What does all of this have to do with dedication? Simply this: *Once a child is old enough to*

*accept Jesus Christ as his Lord and Savior, he
is old enough to accept Jesus Christ's teachings
concerning dedication of his life to full-time Christian service.* He must be challenged with such a
possibility. He must be given an opportunity to
learn more about it, to train for it, to help in any
way possible to practice for it even in childhood
(witnessing to friends, handing out tracts he himself may be able to write, distribute invitations
for services, sing or play for another department
of the Sunday school, become involved in teaching
or assisting a teacher at an early age). He needs
confidence. He needs those who will believe in him
and give him opportunities to become involved in
ministering. Children can be exceptionally willing
and cheerful workers. They can be effective with
their own age group. Give them some love, give
them some guidance, give them some responsibility, give them some encouragement—and they
can accomplish wonders.

Why is it that no one can serve the church
to any great extent until he is white haired or
bald? Why are the deacons, the elders, the trus-
tees, the board chairmen, the Women's Guild
members all "getting along in years"? Are they
more trustworthy because they are more aged?
Are their decisions more right because they are
charter members of the church? Are they able
to handle administrative details more capably than
the younger generation?

Somehow we seem to have large gaps in our
thinking. Or perhaps we are guilty of "cubby-
holing" our thinking in too many matters. Therefore, we come up with a timetable for Christian
living that looks something like this:

Ages   1-5   Play and enjoy yourself
Ages   6-14 Learn about Jesus
Ages 15-25 Dedicate your life to God and train
             for your life's work
Ages 25-65 Work at something you want or have
             to do
Ages 65 ff. Retire and wish for the "good old
             days"

But it's time that we began to update that traditional schedule, for only in Christian circles does it look that way.

Go to India and see a toddler taking care of his younger brother or sister. Watch him help the family, care for the animals, gather dung for cooking and building purposes and prepare for his role as a man in the family. Go to the communists and see how the children are indoctrinated in their "religion" until they are ready, willing and even eager to give their life for the cause.

Or, on the other hand, visit a large United States city where a business meeting is in session. A retired expert in the field is being used as a consultant, to pass his learning and experience on to others who must take up the banner. Or visit a group of men and women who have formed an organization to provide medical or legal services for the poor who could otherwise not receive them. Or seek out some of the men and women who have served their country well in the Armed Forces or in Government positions and are now using several profitable years of their lives, at their own expense or at reduced salaries, to do specific tasks for various agencies.

Again we see the Christian church lagging behind the world at both the top and the bottom of the ladder. We are not allowing our children the opportunity of participating in any form of missionary endeavor (unless they happen to be M.K.'s). Nor are we allowing our older citizens to have a place in Christian ministry. We would do exceedingly well to look to these facts. We need to begin to train our children to be leaders in the Christian cause. Paul had the right idea when he wrote to Timothy, "Let no man despise thy youth; but be thou an example of the believers, in word, in conversation, in charity, in spirit, in faith, in purity" (1 Tim. 4:12).

We also need to take advantage of the talents and abilities of those in and beyond middle age. Why not suggest an early retirement and give an opportunity for meaningful Christian service? Or why should that magical age of 65 denote the receipt of an inscribed gold watch and a reserved room at the retirement center? Not everyone, of course, is physically or financially able to give a few months or years of service out of his own life and pocket. But why hasn't the Christian church volunteered to give support to such projects? Taking on the support of a 24-year-old accepted missionary candidate seems a logical thing to do, even though the candidate may have had little training and no experience. What a fine gesture it would be on the part of the church to send some of its finest and best qualified Christian citizens out to strengthen the hands of the missionaries. There are a thousand jobs to be done, details to be handled, children to be cared for, accounts to be tallied, services to be held for the English-speaking community, items to be repaired, stations to be built and maintained, etc. None of these tasks require so much as learning a new language, unless the individual insists upon doing it in order to have an even wider ministry.

Short-term service is now open to young people of high school age and to men and women of *all* ages. *Why can't we challenge Christians to give at least a tithe of their lives to missionary service?* And why don't we challenge our churches to give at least a tithe of their membership to some form of full-time Christian service? Many churches do well to send 1/10 of 1 percent of their membership into the Lord's service. Some do far less than that!

Yet, the first and greatest Missionary gave a command. To my knowledge, it has never been rescinded; neither has it been fulfilled. It still stands on the books. It is so familiar that most of us read it or listen to it glibly, giving mental assent, and little more.

But a day is coming when we shall stand before God to give an account of the deeds done in the flesh. What will your answer be when He calls your name, looks into your face and asks, "And did *you* go and teach all nations, baptizing them in the name of the Father, and of the Son, and of the Holy Ghost? And did you teach them to observe all things whatsoever I have commanded you?" Will you be ashamed at His voice? Will you cry out in the words of the songwriter, "I wish I had given Him more!" You can, you know. It is not too late to dedicate your life to Him. He isn't interested in your age. He's interested only in your obedience and faithfulness, whether you're 3 or 103!

My friend, dedication is for YOU, if you're a

born-again Christian with a love for God aflame in your heart and a desire to follow in His steps, wherever that may lead. That's who dedication is for!

3

What's To Be Dedicated To?

It was one of the closing speakers at a large missionary conference in the eastern United States who came to grips with a question many must have asked in the quietness of their own heart. There had been many opportunities for dedication of life to missionary service and full-time Christian work. Scores of high school and college-age people had already made that commitment on the first day of the conference when the meetings were geared specifically to their age groups. Now they gathered together in meeting after meeting, hoping to receive a message from heaven concerning how and where they ought to serve.

All week long the figures were given out. The rate of increase in the world population per year compared to the rate of increase in the acceptance of the gospel was mentioned many times. Workers from fields where the work is slow and results have been long in coming to fruition spoke of the need for workers, especially now when souls are, at last, turning to Christ. Others mentioned the size of the communist world and/or the Moslem world in comparison with the Christian world.

We came to realize that some extensive areas of the earth are almost untouched with a gospel witness, while other areas are being saturated by radio, literature, medicine and personal witness.

The films we saw depicted the faces of many peoples in many lands. We saw portrayed before our very eyes the deep poverty of many, the desperate physical needs of others, the struggling heathen, the untaught Christian—those who could neither read nor write, those who were possessed or obsessed by powers unrelated to the gospel of Jesus Christ—lonely workers needing reinforcements—children who had nothing and who might not ever have anything, even if they were fortunate enough to live. We also saw the well-dressed businessmen of the more "sophisticated" areas of the world, lost and dying, but at least living for the present in tolerable circumstances.

We were given literature which, by means of words, pictures, graphs, charts—even cartoons—was intended to show us how much this old world needs the gospel of Jesus Christ.

Our emotions were stirred time and time again as we heard stories, digested figures and viewed slides of the spiritually needy areas of the world.

This well-known annual missionary conference does not, fortunately, depend upon emotions to build up its missions program. But if, after listening to and looking at some of these things, we had been given an opportunity to move down the aisles to dedicate our lives to missionary service, many of us would have pushed others out of the way to make sure of being at the head of the line of volunteers.

Now suppose we had done just that. To what

would we have been dedicating our lives? I'm
afraid in many cases it would have been for the
purpose of making a graph look better; or filling
a gap in a particular situation; or wrestling with
the powers of darkness to prove that the blood
of Christ overcomes all obstacles; or lightening
the load of an overworked missionary; or making
use of an ability that may or may not have been
in demand here at home; or to show others that
we were willing to put aside worldly ambitions
and the pursuit of money in order to assist the
missions program of the church; or to prove to
ourselves that we were willing to go if the Lord
should call (even though we sincerely doubted
that He would); or to fulfill a desire for challenge,
adventure and travel; or we might have been
overly impressed with the speaker and expressed
it by volunteering; or perhaps we had been considering service but hadn't previously declared it
openly.

We could go on, but there is no reason to do
so. Many of these reasons are certainly valid
motives for dedicating one's life to full-time Christian service. Or *are* they?

Read over the list above once more. Check
off those you feel have truly valid motivation for
dedication.

Now remember, our question is, "What are we
dedicated to?" And that missionary stood on the
platform, looking down at the congregation, and
said, "I'm afraid we are too dedicated to charts,
graphs and figures while the only valid motivation
for full-time service is devotion to the Lord Jesus
Christ."

Is that a new thought? It ought not to be. And

yet how many Christian workers have gone forth
for other reasons! How many have chosen a
mission field because the workers were few? "If
you had to move a log, and there were nine men
on one end and only one on the other, which group
would you help?" That was the question often
put to those who wanted to be missionaries. Or
we were told, "Ninety percent of the people live
in rural areas, but 90 percent of the missionaries
work in the cities." So the idea was to become
dedicated to the down-country areas.

Oh, it's important that those who dedicate
themselves for Christian service know the needs
of the people of the world, that they be informed
concerning facts and figures; that they be apprised
of the dangers of certain areas and the shortness
of time in others, even though neither may actually be factual; that they know if their talents will
fulfill a ministry in a particular field. But Christian work is more than meeting a certain quota
or reaching a specified people. If poverty and
sickness are the criteria for dedication, it is
not enough. If a need for workers or a supply
of financial aid are the criteria for dedication, it
is not enough. If your talents and abilities suit
you for a particular service in a particular place
and these are your criteria for dedication, they are
not enough. The only criteria which is valid for
dedicating your life for Christian service is your
love for and obedience to the Lord Jesus Christ.

He himself made it very plain to us. He used
simple words. He made it easy for us to understand. And yet we insist on something more difficult, more complicated—yes, perhaps more sophisticated. It reminds us of dear Naaman. He longed

so very much to be rid of his leprosy. He was intelligent, a leader, a mighty man—but he was a leper. When the Syrians had gone out, they took a little girl captive out of Israel. She was assigned the responsibility of being maid to Naaman's wife. The little girl felt desperately sorry for Naaman, and one day she chanced to say, "If only my lord could visit the prophet Elisha in Samaria. He could be made well." Someone overheard her and carried her remark to the king of Syria. For some strange reason—probably because he was willing to grasp at any straw in order to relieve Naaman of his sickness—the king believed the word of the maid.

The king of Syria didn't go directly to Naaman, however. Instead he sent word, in a letter, to the king of Israel, and also sent a great sum of money, asking him to heal Naaman of his leprosy. The king of Israel was overcome by the request and managed to say, "Am I God?"

Elisha, the prophet, heard about this, and went to the king, and promised to help Naaman. When Naaman arrived, Elisha didn't so much as go to the door to greet him. Instead, he sent a messenger who told Naaman, "Go and wash in Jordan seven times, and thy flesh shall come again to thee, and thou shalt be clean."

The orders were simple; the command was clear; the words were easily understood. But rather than stepping out by faith on Elisha's promise through his messenger, Naaman became extremely angry. He was disappointed that Elisha hadn't come to him in person. And he was disgusted at the thought of dipping in the dirty Jordan River.

"Why, we've got far better rivers in Damascus. Why shouldn't I dip in them and be made clean?" he asked. And he turned away in a rage.

He hadn't gone far when his servants spoke to him saying, "If the prophet had commanded you to do some outstanding thing, you surely would have done it. Why won't you obey his simple words and go wash seven times in the Jordan?"

Naaman must have felt thoroughly rebuked by their words, for he then went down to the Jordan, obeyed the simple command, and God cleansed him from his leprosy (see 2 Kings 5).

Are we as dedicated to serving Christ as Naaman was dedicated to being free of his leprosy? If so, Jesus speaks some very simple words to us: "Thou shalt love the Lord thy God with all thy heart, and with all thy soul, and with all thy mind. This is the first and great commandment. And the second is like unto it, Thou shalt love thy neighbour as thyself" (Matt. 22:37-39).

This is God's divinely appointed order. Nowhere in Scripture do we find these commandments reversed. Dedicating your life to Christian service out of love for your fellowman is, indeed, a worthy purpose. But it must not be the primary calling for dedication. Love for God must be the foremost motivation for dedication to His service. Anything less is, at best, God's second best. Thus we come to see what's to be dedicated to!

4

What Do Dedicated People Do?

It is entirely possible that in a moment when
the Holy Spirit was at work in a life, the individual
was moved to dedicate his life for Christian service. Having taken this step, his next logical question might well be, "But what does a full-time
Christian worker actually do?" This is an important consideration for two reasons:

1. Young people will need to prepare for a
specific area of service.

2. Older people will need to know if their
background, training, experience and abilities
can be used in full-time service at home or
overseas.

Today we live in an era of specialization. There
was a time when a scientist spent his lifetime in
the study of fruit flies. Today the scientist spends
his lifetime in the study of the hairs on the leg
of a fruit fly! This same correlation exists in
Christian work, especially in the area of missions.
A missionary once went to the field as a generalist, supposedly knowledgeable in any and/or
all facets of endeavor. Today the missionary,

more and more, goes to the field as a specialist in his profession. This does not take away from the fact that he is first and foremost obedient to Jesus Christ as His witness wherever he may be. But it does control the acceptance of unlimited numbers of those who have no special training (beyond a good knowledge of the Word of God). Missions which have, in the past, taken on a large number of "general" missionaries are, today, finding it difficult to place them in strategic locations on the field. Legislation (both at home and overseas) is demanding higher qualifications and training for workers. Continuing education requirements for medical workers, teachers and other professionals is cause for limiting the assigned tasks of unskilled workers. The day is quickly passing when a generalist can automatically practice as a teacher in the School for Missionary Children, or even in a mission-operated national school.

As nations have arisen and declared their independence, they have also begun to decide what missionaries can and cannot do within their borders. Some have come to the decision that missionaries are something they can do very well without. Others are demanding that the missionary be used in advisory, supervisory and administrative positions. Thus, he who once went from village to village with Bible in hand, preaching and teaching as time and occasion permitted, is now forced into a position where he must train nationals for this task. Nurses, who once cared for patients and handled reports, are now teaching nationals to perform in this capacity. National teachers, preachers, evangelists, medical workers, printers, musicians, translators, etc., are being trained for positions of leadership. Once trained, some have been able to take over large segments of the work formerly manned and administered by the foreigner. This seems to be a scriptural method of fulfilling God's plan. According to 2 Timothy 2:2, Paul's advice to Timothy was this: "And the things that thou hast heard of me among many witnesses, the same commit thou to faithful men, who shall be able to teach others also." If, from the beginning, missionaries had trained nationals, allowed them to carry on the work when they were able, and then moved on to new areas, the world would have long since been reached with the gospel. Unfortunately, in too many places we have not been content to teach, preach and baptize, and then leave the leadership to the national constituency. It is true that in some situations this was not possible. People had to be taught a trade, or agriculture, to eliminate their need to live by raiding neighboring tribes. Many missionaries have not understood the people among whom they work, and have sought to impose upon them western civilization which, in their teaching, they have equated with Christian living. Thus, they have not felt the nationals have come to that point of being ready to separate themselves from the oversight of the foreign missionary.

But in many situations, proper instruction, establishment of Bible training schools, establishment of churches and opportunities for national witness would have been suitable goals for the missionaries.

It is too late to unravel that which has been

knit into the fiber of missionary work worldwide. But it is obvious that missions are taking a second look at the whole matter of missionary service, and they are coming up with new policies, procedures and patterns for more useful and effective ministry overseas. They are also challenging nationals to missionary service, not only within their own borders, but in other countries of the world as well.

Within the changing kaleidoscope of missionary endeavor, we are beginning to see the need for specialists who can assist the nationals in getting the gospel to their own people in this mechanized and modern day in which we live.

You mean missionaries no longer simply preach the Word of God 24 hours a day and 7 days a week? This is exactly what we are trying to say. You see, unfortunately, a missionary "image" has been passed on to our generation. It is a picture of a white male, dressed in a white shirt, white shorts, knee socks and a pith helmet, Bible in hand, standing under a palm tree, preaching to almost-naked, dark-skinned, unlearned people who live in round grass huts. During four years of missionary service in West Pakistan, I saw this "image" just once (and even then the nationals were fully clothed and they lived in square mud homes with straw roofs)!

So what do dedicated people do overseas? The answer is fairly uncomplicated. They perform the same types of ministries that people in the homeland perform. They assist in getting the gospel to the greatest number of people in the best possible way. Their lives are a testimony to the

Lord Jesus Christ 24 hours a day and 7 days a week. But wasn't the Lord's last command to us to "Go . . . teach . . . preach . . . baptize"? Yes, it was. Is the task completed? No! Could it be accomplished in our generation? Yes, it could. Will it be? Probably not. Why? Because we still expect that a few "general" missionaries are going to be able to win the world for Christ. We are still "pedestalizing" missionaries, considering them as super-human individuals who, through great personal sacrifice and loss, and the giving up of everything near and dear to them, will expend themselves on behalf of a tribe or a nation committed to their responsibility.

When I went to West Pakistan as a missionary, I was part of a force of approximately 400 who were seeking to win the largest Muslim Republic in the world to Christ. With an estimated population of 40,000,000 souls to contend with, each of us assumed that his responsibility amounted to 100,000 souls. That's quite a parish—and an utter impossibility! The Lord Jesus Christ touched the lives of many thousands during His brief 33 years on earth, and specifically during His 3 years of public ministry. But His main ministry during His lifetime (apart from His life-giving death and resurrection) was to teach 12 chosen men, none of whom had any extraordinary ability or potential.

We have so many means at our disposal that were not available in our Lord's day upon the earth. By making use of those means, our ministry can be extended and enhanced a thousand-fold. It is unfortunate that while the world has been advancing at a dizzying pace, missions have continued to carry out their work with outmoded men, machines and methods—until recently. At last we are beginning to wake up and utilize the means at our disposal to bring Christ to a lost and darkened world. But in so doing, we must also utilize men and women who are well versed in the application and extension of these means so that the ultimate result will be the salvation of souls and the building up of the body of Christ. This, after all, is the only valid goal of missionary endeavor, which, when brought to fruition, fulfills the command of our Lord.

With this in mind, let's consider some of those areas of service which are open to those who would dedicate their lives to missionary service.

EVANGELISM AND CHURCH GROWTH

Preaching
Teaching
Child Evangelism
Camps
Pastoral consultation
Establishing churches

Personal evangelism
Counseling
Gospel team efforts
Musical ministries
Youth work
General missionary work

EDUCATION

Elementary/Secondary/College
    teacher
Bible School/Seminary teacher
School for Missionary Children
Teaching English as a second
    language
Library work
Continuing education

Education counselor
Christian education work
Teacher training
Extension education
Adult education
Administration/supervision

COMMUNICATIONS

Radio/TV personnel

Engineering

Printing
Record librarians
Literature production/
    distribution
Lay-out workers
Bookstore management
Correspondence courses
Writing/scripts/journalism

Art
Statisticians
Photography/films
Editing
Follow-up
Proofreaders
Researchists
Technicians

MEDICINE

Doctors/surgeons
Nurses
Pharmacists
Medical technicians
Medical secretaries
Publich Health workers
Nutritionists/dieticians
Continuing education
Hospital administrators
Nursing supervisors
Opthalmologists
Anaesthesiologists

Mid-wives
Radiologists
Medical librarians
X-ray technicians
Dentists
Dental technicians
Physical therapists
Occupational therapists
Lab technicians
School of
    Nursing personnel

SOCIAL SERVICES

Agriculture
Forestry
Sociology
Industrial engineers
Counseling

Child care
Physical education
Family planning personnel
Veterinarians
Builders

BUSINESS

File clerks
Travel advisors
Accountants
Bookkeepers
Public Relations
Personnel management
Administration

Secretary/office workers
Typists
Writers
Shipping
Purchasing
Distribution of supplies
Business management

SUPPORT MINISTRIES

Construction engineering	Maintenance workers
Architectural engineering	Researchists/analysists
Aviation	Hostess/hospitality
Transportation	House parents
Mechanics	Rest home managers
Linguists	Literacy workers
Ham radio operators	Civil/mechanical/chemical
Electricians	engineering

Does the fact that a missionary goes by one of the foregoing professional titles make him less than a missionary? No, of course not! The emphasis of his work may be different from the time-worn image we have of him. But his *raison d'etre* remains the same: to fulfill our Lord's last command, namely, " . . . ye shall be witnesses unto me both in Jerusalem, and in all Judea, and in Samaria, and unto the uttermost part of the earth" (Acts 1:8).

In his book, *Winds of Change in the Christian Mission* (Moody Press, 1973), Dr. J. Herbert Kane vividly points out that missionaries are no longer thought of as heroes. We live in a day when men and women volunteer for any number of jobs overseas—in industry, in government service, in the Armed Forces, in the Peace Corps, with the World Health Organization, etc., Vacationing in Europe, taking a world cruise, or signing up for an African safari are everyday experiences about which we read continually. There is no longer anything magical about going across the ocean. As far as the missionary is concerned, the nationals are not lining the gate when his plane pulls in; there is usually no large delegation to see him off as he flies out again. Nor is an unduly big crowd awaiting his arrival in the homeland. He is just another worker doing the job he volunteered for and dedicated his life to. He is called a missionary because he is "one sent" to witness of the truth of the gospel to other people.

If an individual goes forth with the sole purpose in mind of practicing his profession as an end in itself, he is not a "missionary" of the cross in the Christian interpretation and definition of the term. Only as his main purpose in life and the primary thrust of his work is directed toward helping in the propagation of the faith, doctrine and principles of Christian living, as described in the Word of God, is the individual suitably called a "missionary."

You have dedicated your life to a commitment to Christian service. You have declared your willingness to do God's will, whatever that will might entail. Perhaps you are not sure, even yet, what service you may be able to render, but you should at least be aware of some of the things that dedicated people do!

5

Is Dedication Only for
Foreign Service?

Responding to an invitation to dedication, even at the close of a missionary conference, does not obligate an individual to service among a primitive, cannibalistic tribe on foreign soil. The initial giving of oneself in this act of dedication should be prefaced by a willingness to seek and follow the guidance of God in every area of life. If the response was to a definite call of missionary volunteers, you must carefully and prayerfully consider your calling. It is easy to lay hold of God in a moment when all barriers have been broken down by the Spirit of God. It is far more difficult to let God lay hold of *you* in those days and weeks following that decision.

But does a missionary call automatically imply foreign service? We have been told that all Christians are one of two things, namely, (1) a missionary, or (2) a mission field. This is a "general" call to all who name the Name of Christ. But even this does not set apart every believer to full-time overseas service. If all Christians were deployed to foreign posts, the homeland would find itself in a pitiful state. God works things decently and orderly. We have only to look at the variety of His creative genius to realize He never intended for all of us to be appointed to one particular station in life.

In the book of Acts, we have a good example of what must be done if we are to get the gospel out effectively. The disciples had dedicated their lives to full-time preaching. It occurred to them that it should not be their responsibility to take care of supplying provisions to the needy in their midst. Therefore, others from among the Christians were dedicated to that purpose. Although it was a *different* responsibility, it was not considered a *lesser* one. The men having been chosen, and having shown a willingness to commit themselves to the appointed task, they were ordained to that ministry by prayer and the laying on of hands. This freed the disciples for full-time service in prayer and the ministry of the Word (see Acts 6:1-7).

Definite dedication to a specific sphere of service on the part of some must be accompanied by the willingness of other dedicated workers to a ministry of support and helpfulness. You may be willing to be a missionary. But God may have something else planned for you where your background, education, experience, talents and abilities can be used to their greatest extent. Too many people have been told, "If God has called you to be a missionary, never stoop to be a king (or queen)." Then when health, circumstances or other situations forced the volunteer to give up plans for overseas service, he felt as though he had failed God; and in many instances, feeling he was only doing God's second best, has become embittered, powerless, useless, or over-zealous in other service, resulting in physical, emotional or mental breakdown, or a life lived in regret over a supposedly broken promise.

Undoubtedly, there are thousands who have responded to the call to dedication for missionary service or full-time Christian work who have not entered it, and should have; others have moved forward when they shouldn't have. But the call of God is a personal call; it demands a personal response; it requires a personal dedication; and it requires a personal fulfillment. No one can make this important decision for another. It is as individual as the call to salvation; it is also as universal. And in the same manner, there will be those who dedicated their lives for Christian service because it seemed the thing to do, they were convinced by words, their friends responded, they were forced into it, it was expected of them; and there will be those who truly sense that God is setting them apart for His service.

Suppose now that your response was to an invitation to "dedicate your life to God for full-time service." Does that necessitate preparation for and service in an overseas setting? Not at all. It should be a means of declaring that you are willing for such a ministry if God indicates it to be His will in Christ Jesus concerning you. And you should earnestly consider it as a legitimate fulfillment of your commitment.

But there are other areas of full-time service which need dedicated workers, too. There are certainly no restrictions on the breadth of ministries to be rendered in the homeland. Home missionaries, pastors, teachers in Christian institutions, workers in missionary-oriented organizations, ghetto workers, child evangelism ministers, youth workers, musical teams, personal evangelists, street meeting workers, tract distributors, Christian writers/editors, broadcasters, home Bible study group leaders, Christian Education directors, Rescue Mission directors, Prison evangelists, Christian counselors, camp workers, Bible conference managers, ministry of opening closed churches, Gideon work, Christian Nurses' Fellowship, ministries to foreign students and visitors, and we could go on and on naming ministries which can be carried out without ever leaving your present location (except as schooling needs might necessitate).

Dedicating one's life for full-time Christian overseas service, although there is a real possibility that God's will may lead in that direction, is not implicit in a commitment in dedication of your life to the Lord for full-time service. America is not yet Christian in the pure sense of the word. We must maintain a strong supply base at home if we are to reach out with any real effectiveness overseas.

6

After Dedication, What?

It is almost always a time of rejoicing when a large group of individuals surges forward in response to the call for dedication to full-time Christian service. (There may be a few parents who are unwilling to "give up" their children for even such a high and holy calling.) The usual service of dedication ends with a final call for "anyone who would still like to join the group." Then a closing prayer and the service is dismissed. Now what happens to the 8-year-old or the 16-year-old— or the 60-year-old who made an honest commitment to God in this call to dedication? Is he left to shift for himself and seek to find a scripture verse, or a message in the sky, or to work out his uncertain circumstances in such a way that the will of God will become reasonably sure to him? It sounds absurd when you read these things in print, but isn't that what usually happens?

There is a large area of responsibility where the church has taken little time and had inadequate concern. There has been little or no follow-up among those who have honestly and sincerely dedicated their lives to God for full-time service. There may have been great rejoicing over a few decisions; others may have been taken with a grain of salt; yet others did what had been expected they would do. For the moment, statistics will be the thing folks will remember about the service. Who wouldn't be pleased to say, "Last night, 35 young people dedicated their lives to the Lord for full-time service!"

But what happens during the weeks and months after this decision is made public? Usually nothing. Most of the adults in the congregation won't be concerned again with this matter until next year's missionary conference. Then they'll silently say, "Well, so and so won't be going forward this year because she did that *last* year!" And the young people who responded may not think too much about it until next year's conference, and when the invitation is given for dedication they will respond silently, "I don't have to go forward this year because I did it *last* year."

I am thoroughly convinced that the Christian Church must begin a program of follow-through if it is going to expect young people, and older folks, to respond to a dedication invitation. Lack of such follow-through has resulted in the eventual loss of at least 80 percent of those who at one point in their lifetime made that all-important decision to serve the Lord full time. In fact, some statisticians have implied that only 1 out of every 100 volunteers ever gets to the mission field. Whether there is any factual research available on this, or not, is questionable. Nevertheless, from our own knowledge, we must agree that there is an excessively high drop-out rate among those who once affirmed their desire to "go to the ends of the earth with the gospel," if—and that is a very important IF—if the Lord should so lead.

But what kind of follow-through can be established in order to conserve the majority of these decisions? There is much that can be done, and in these pages we shall only begin to present all that can be done to encourage not only those who have already responded to the challenge, but also those who, in the future, will walk down that aisle.

It is important that a church consider what lies beyond dedication before a pastor, missionary, or guest preacher gives an invitation for full-time service. The invitation is the beginning of a far-reaching, extended experience. It is important that it should come from only those who have been rightly related to God through faith in the redemptive work of Jesus Christ. Since dedication is first of all a full-time commitment to Him rather than to a task, it follows that only those who belong to Him can dedicate their lives to serving Him. The better they know Him, the more meaningful their dedication will be. The longer they know Him, the stronger should be their desire to fulfill His will.

There are hundreds of thousands of believers who trust the Savior. The number of those who own Him as Lord are considerably fewer. They *call* Him Savior and Lord, but the proof of this truth is found only in living. And it is all too evident that most of us do not accept, understand, or benefit from the lordship of Christ. Our own wills are too demanding; our own ways are too alluring. It is regrettable that we are willing to accept the Way of Life to provide us only with the assurance of heaven. God provided

Life for us to enjoy here and now . . . and forever. Why do we continue to insist on struggling with our own plans, problems and programs when He wants to order our steps and direct our paths? Why do we call Him King of kings and Lord of lords and yet neither commit ourselves to Him or obey Him? Why are our lives, too often, powerless and fruitless? The answer is simple. We refuse to be infused with the power of the Holy Spirit, who is willing and able to lead us into all truth. We refuse to accept our total life needs from eating of the Living Bread and drinking of the Living Water. And God cannot and will not bless fence walkers. He makes it very clear what He thinks of lukewarmness—those who walk with one foot in heaven and one in the world; those who, at their own will, accept His word when it is compatible to their thinking, and otherwise rely upon their own judgment or the advice of other men. God says He can't swallow such living. His exact words to the church at Laodicea, in which He told them He recognized this as their condition, are: "I will spue thee out of my mouth" (Rev. 3:16).

God doesn't say, "Be holy when you feel like being holy." He commands, "Be ye holy, for I am holy" (1 Pet. 1:16). We try to get around such statements with various excuses: "None of us will be perfect in this life," "God really meant something quite different," or "He really had the Old Testament saints in mind when He said that." I am declaring unto you that God always says what He means and means what He says! And if we trust Him—and we say we do—and if we obey Him—and we say we do—and if we are His servants—and we say we are—then where has the lordship of Jesus Christ gone?

It is the responsibility of those in the home church to believe and teach the lordship of Christ. If this truth is ignored, there will be little interest in dedication to full-time service.

Hopefully, you are a strong believer in the authenticity of your young people and in their willingness to seek God's will and do it. Your very attitude toward this decision is vitally important, and your continuing confidence and helpfulness will preserve the fruits which have been produced.

First of all, each one who offers himself for full-time Christian service should be personally commended by the church, and particularly by the pastor. A conference should be set up either at the church office or in the home. This should not be a formal and embarrassing situation, but rather a brief encounter so that the individual will come to appreciate the pastor's interest in being as helpful as possible, and the pastor will understand what the individual had in mind when he walked the aisle. Ignoring the fact that a life-changing decision has been attested to will cause the individual to feel that what he did was unimportant, unnoticed and unnecessary.

Once each individual has been interviewed, group sessions should be established at a time convenient to all who will attend. Groups will do best if established by general age categories. The pastor may not be able to meet personally with each group, but others within the congregation should be encouraged to volunteer for this ministry—perhaps a Christian worker, a missionary, a member of the local body of believers who loves the Lord and is interested in His work, a church leader, the Christian Education Director—but those who are chosen must fully understand what their task is and seek to fulfill it to the best of their abilities.

It may be that one Sunday a month has already been set aside as Missionary Day in the Sunday school. If so, on that day those who have dedicated their lives for service may meet with their group leader for instruction, questions and answers, information or service. This will keep their interest active.

What should be done in these sessions? There are far too many options to list here, but certainly there should be some solid teaching given concerning those things which will strengthen the individual's dedication decision. All teaching should be related to daily living and not just to "what you may be doing in the future." Information should be given to the greatest possible extent. This will, of course, include as much as possible concerning opportunities for long-term service, short-term service, ministries in the homeland, missionary work overseas and at home, pastoral work, Christian Education opportunities, etc. Literature (brochures, books, magazines, pamphlets and other material) should be made available either on an individual basis or through the church library. Many Christian organizations, bookstores and publishing houses will be able to supply you with written materials of many kinds.

Schooling is a definite consideration for teenagers who must prepare themselves in a specialty. The pro's and con's of secular versus Christian education must be discussed. Catalogs from as wide a variety of schools as possible should be made available, including those from universities, colleges, schools of nursing, Bible schools, technical institutes, specialized courses, etc. If an individual has an interest in a particular field, he should know where to get information regarding that specialty. Inasmuch as possible, Christian leaders in the fields of interest within the group should be invited to share in a meeting. Being able to ask questions of experienced and knowledgeable people will go far toward making certain avenues of ministry more meaningful.

It would be of tremendous help to assist each individual in setting goals for the future. Most young people know nothing about setting priorities. With the help of both the group itself and its advisor, reachable goals can be set in keeping with the ultimate goals having to do with involvement in full-time service.

Enthusiasm should be generated within the group. Reports of Christian missions and organizations should be a constant source of inspiration and fuel for prayer. It should be emphasized that full-time service for Jesus Christ is a full and rewarding experience. It does not mean giving up the best in life. It is a pinpointing of the best, enhancement of it and its utilization to the highest degree. It is not "sissy" work. It requires the highest and best.

Included in the group sessions should be short courses geared to the interests of the group. Some of the topics should include an overview of basic Christianity, comparative religions, history of missions, world problems, geography, witnessing, how to teach, witness, maintain victory, stand tests, resist temptation, know the will of God, be rightly related to self and others, etc.

As soon as an individual is dedicated for full-time service, it would be extremely helpful if he/she were assigned a big brother or big sister from among the people of the congregation. Individuals interested in helping a young person in the church could volunteer for this specific ministry. Their responsibility would be a prayer fellowship for (and perhaps with) the teen-ager. The volunteer could be assigned the responsibility of assisting in obtaining materials from schools and/or mission boards, or helping the young person find adequate resources. If the family of the one who has dedicated his life for service is a Christian family, it is possible that they will give a good deal of guidance and assistance. It will depend to a large extent on the rapport which exists within the family group. Sometimes a family deals more effectively with those outside the family circle, or may wish to include others with nonsupportive or non-Christian parents in their counseling of their own young people.

All of these things should be done, as much as possible, with the full consent of both parents and young people. It would be a poor testimony to the family and a harmful experience to the young person if he were forced to pursue the matter of full-time service if he should come to the point where he cannot truthfully continue to go in that direction. Honesty on the part of all concerned, a climate in which things can be freely discussed and an acknowledgment on the part of the participants concerning their true attitudes and feelings about these sessions will add to their effectiveness.

Every opportunity should be given these young people, no matter how old they are, to serve in a particular capacity, especially suited to them. There is no limit on the amount of involvement possible within the ministries in and outreach of the church. Prayer, testimony, music (vocal or instrumental), Scripture reading, library helper, teacher's aide, tract distributor, bulletin writer, usher, greeter, representative to the Christian Education Committee, planning a missionary Sunday or conference for children and young people, visitation, etc., are possible ways to utilize the dedication of these youngsters. Missionaries are not made by crossing an ocean. They begin by serving at home. It is important that they be given as many opportunities as possible. Guidance can be provided. Evaluations can be made. Advice may be shared.

When the young person goes away to school, his big brother should maintain constant contact with him by corresponding, sending news of and bulletins from the church, sending a gift parcel as a special treat once in a while, phone calls. Cards should be sent for holidays and special days. It would be of much encouragement if financial help could be given by the church (if only $50 or $100 per year). Many times the men's and/or women's group set up a special fund for just such a purpose. Sometimes during the Opening Worship of Adult Sunday School, a "praise bank" is used to gather money. If folks are thankful for God's special blessing on them, they put an offering in the bank and give a short word of testimony. This money could be used for those training for full-time service. There may be individuals in the congregation who would assist in a Project Fund for the purpose of providing funds for church young people training for full-time service.

The church as a whole should be kept informed concerning those in training for His service.

Names and addresses should be placed in the bulletin periodically as reminders to pray and write. Reports should be given periodically in church, prayer meeting, young people's meetings and/or Sunday school. When they are home for the summer or holidays, they should be recognized and utilized in the services. Being used in the home church is an internship experience which should be afforded all those who would serve their Lord.

If, during the course of his studies, the young person determines he will go to the mission field, it should be the responsibility of the home church to support him in his endeavor. This should be true also for those who carry on ministries at home which require the support of God's people. This includes not only a willingness to assist with information, or utilization of his services, but financial support as well.

This, perhaps, is one of the final tests of the interest of the church in its own young people. Too many times the missionary volunteer is expected to find his support from strangers near and far. The church feels no obligation in this regard. Brethren, this ought not so to be! But it is, indeed, a good thermometer of the interest the church has in the dedicated Christian service of its own people.

The church has a tremendous responsibility to those who dedicate themselves for full-time service. It must bear the burden of prayer, encouragement, teaching, involvement, ministering to needs, financial help, counseling, guidance and fellowship.

And for those who are older and dedicate themselves to full-time service, these same principles apply. They should receive the same type of assistance from their fellow church members. They should find ready and willing counsel and reputable advice. Some may be able to take an early retirement from their work to give time in Christian service. Others may be retired, but can be used in any number of capacities in a large number of areas. Financially, there is the possibility that these folks can be self-supporting. If not, and the church has confidence in them, they should receive financial assistance from the home church. Surely this is the first and foremost obligation of the missions program in any church—to care for its own people, dedicated to serving Christ.

What have we been trying to say? There is far more to dedication than walking down an aisle. The church must be willing to develop a program of training for those who make this decision. There must be serious cooperation between the pastor, the congregation and the volunteers. Ample opportunity must be given for serving the Lord within the home church. Guidance should be available as needed. Encouragement should be evident. An Advisory Committee may need to be appointed to work out the details of how to deal effectively with every facet of the educational continuum. A new item may need to be added to the annual budget, i.e., support for those in training for full-time Christian service. A further item may then be required, namely support for your very own missionaries, born, raised and nurtured in the home church.

If and when any or all of these suggestions become part of an ongoing program in the church, there will be no question in the minds of those who have walked down the aisle when the next call to dedication for full-time service rolls around—probably at next year's missionary conference. Those who have made the decision will have no need to make that decision again, but others who have watched with interest all that has been done on behalf of those volunteers may be more anxious to give themselves to the service of Christ knowing that they will not be forgotten as soon as the meeting has been dismissed.

What if there is only one person who goes forward when the invitation to dedication is given? Should that one be neglected because he is only one? Not at all. Every possible assistance should be given him in an atmosphere of friendship, helpfulness and Christian love. It is possible that his commitment will reach through to others who will be willing to make a decision also.

We keep speaking of the invitation to dedication which is given from a pulpit. We would be remiss if we did not assure the reader that just as salvation can be received informally, outside the walls of a church building, so dedication of one's life to full-time Christian commitment can become a reality in the same way. If such a commitment is made, the church should be made aware of it so they can share in the privilege of providing all possible help, guidance and assistance. But this decision does not necessarily come at a specified time in a formal way under the direction of an ordained speaker.

Does anything come after dedication? In looking back it might be more accurate to ask, did anything ever come *before* dedication? This experience ought to give new life and dimension to the entire program and outreach of your church. It may be the start of a dedication to Christ and His service unparalleled with any previous experience in your church. May this be so!

7

Does Dedication Last?

After a person has walked the aisle to dedicate his life to full-time Christian service, perhaps one of the first questions that jumps to mind is, but will it last?

This, of course, is a difficult question to answer. No one truly knows the mind and purpose of another human being but God himself. Did Jane go forward because her boyfriend did? Did Bill go forward because his parents are missionaries and it is logical for him to indicate his willingness to go too? What were the many reasons for these decisions? Were they real? Will they last?

The Lord Jesus Christ spent the major part of His public ministry training twelve men. He took them as He found them and accepted them for what they were. They seemed to be dedicated to serving Him. They sat at His feet and learned of Him. They asked Him questions. They saw Him perform miracles. They listened as He spoke to the multitudes. They enjoyed His presence and fellowship. They declared their allegiance to Him.

And how did they turn out? Did their dedication last? We have the advantage of looking back over the full length of their lives. At times, did we not know the entire story, we would have to say that their dedication did not last. Surely if we were to ask that question as Jesus was being tried for His very life, we would conclude that their dedication was meaningless, for they all forsook Him and fled (except Peter, who not only followed afar off, but also denied Him vehemently on at least three occasions).

But we must look beyond the mountain-top and valley experiences of their lives to find our answer. And therein we discover that Judas was the only one whose dedication to the Lord did not last. In the book of Acts we discover the other disciples fulfilling their commitment to Jesus Christ by the giving of themselves to Him in service.

There may be times when that walk down the aisle seems to have been a waste. In the ups and downs of human experience it may appear that there is little hope that some of these lives can be or will be used of God in Christian service.

Perhaps our reasoning comes from the fact that we have forgotten that dedication is made real only through the sealing of the Holy Spirit of God. It is the Spirit that keeps what we commit to God. He it is who leads and guides us into all truth. He is the one who takes the prayers of our hearts and makes them intelligible to our heavenly Father. He prods us to holy living. He maintains in us a consciousness of the claims of Christ upon our lives. If we honestly, earnestly dedicate ourselves to Christian service, He will strengthen our convictions and bring us to a knowledge of God's will for our lives. He stands beside us to encourage and enlighten. He gives needed wisdom. He supplies every need.

Does dedication last? There is every reason why it should. If it doesn't, there is every reason to believe that the blame rests upon us and not upon God. I have known children who at the early age of 5 or 6 have knowingly determined to become servants for the Master. Twenty years later they were in the ministry or on the mission field. God had adequately kept their decision before them, and they had obeyed His desires for them. I have known others who walked down an aisle at the age of 18 or 20 who six months or six weeks later had completely forgotten their decision. Follow-up could certainly have had a great deal to do with establishing these decisions in an environment of growth and development. But the individual must surely bear the major responsibility if dedication is to last.

What does the sealing of the Holy Spirit actually accomplish? We all know what an official seal means on an important document. A Last Will and Testament has a seal placed upon it to indicate its validity. A Notary Public establishes the authenticity of legal signatures by embossing his seal upon them. When one receives a high school diploma or college degree, the seal of the school is firmly imprinted to attest to the fact that what is written on the parchment is true and that the individual did, in truth, finish a certain segment of his education.

In this same sense, after an individual dedicates his life to Christian service, the Holy Spirit sets His seal upon that life to indicate the truth, validity and authenticity of that commitment. This sealing also indicates His willingness to stand behind His Name in helping us to fulfill God's purpose for our life.

If, then, there is a reliance upon the Spirit of God to fulfill His work, there should be no reason to ask if dedication lasts. Under such conditions, it must!

8

Is There More To Be Said About

"Full-Time" Service?

In a previous chapter we have made it quite clear that dedication to full-time Christian service can include service at home or abroad. We mentioned several categories of endeavor which might be chosen as Christian careers. Although a "lay person" may be as fully dedicated to serving the Lord as those who serve as "professional Christian workers," we have a tendency to limit our concept of "full-time Christian workers" to those few overworked and underpaid missionaries of the cross serving in substandard living conditions, receiving substandard wages, and doing superhuman work. The day may be coming, however, when it may be understood that there are millions of "full-time Christian workers" in the world.

Just a few short years ago, I worked in the home office of a missionary organization. I remember going to a missionary banquet one evening, and as part of the introduction the leader said, "Will all of you who are in full-time Christian work please stand?" I was not among those who stood.

Why? Because I was on the staff of the organization which I served. I was paid, not from designated funds, but from the general fund of the mission. I was not a member of the organization, because I was not classed as a "missionary." And on other occasions I had been informed that all of this meant just one thing: I was not really a full-time Christian worker.

Today, if the same question were put to me, I would stand. Am I a missionary? No. I'm a full-time, free-lance Christian writer. But as such, my full time is given to Christian service, albeit not in the traditional definition of the word.

More and more we are coming to understand a very simple fact. A born-again believer is a Christian. A Christian who works is a worker. If a Christian, in his work—whatever that work might be—seeks to give his life to God, but works to earn a living within a secular setting, he can still be classed as a Christian worker, and hopefully he considers it a full-time ministry to maintain his witness for Jesus Christ. Paul fell into this category, for he supported his own ministry by making tents.

These are the unsung heroes of the Christian faith who lovingly support missionaries with their prayers and financial help; they devote as much time as possible to teaching young people, or older ones, in the things of the Lord; their very lives—what they do, what they say, what they are—speaks loudly of a dedication to Jesus Christ which may be more convincing than a mere recital of what God's Word says. These are the chosen few who stay at home to hold the ropes while others enlarge the place of their tents, lengthen the

cords and strengthen the stakes (Isa. 54:2). Just
as God uses support ministries in His work overseas, He uses them in every place. Whether lay-
man or clergyman, he has a share in the harvest.
Whether nurse, business executive, administrator,
janitor, farmer, or any one of a thousand other
things, he must make his calling and election sure.
Once that has been determined, he should dedicate
his life to God's highest and best purposes in the
field in which he chooses to serve.

There is a fine line of distinction here between
what can be considered God's call and what we
consider we ought to do with our lives. Is it true
that God calls all of us to missionary service overseas? We have already established the fallacy
of such reasoning. If, indeed, God's call were of
such a nature, every Ethiopian believer would have
to leave Ethiopia, every Indian believer would have
to leave India, etc., in order to fulfill Christ's last
command. But it is absolutely imperative that every born-again believer be assured that he allows
God an opportunity to intervene in his life to such
an extent that there will be no doubt of God's
will for him. Excuses are easy to find or make
up. We can warp and twist sensible reasoning.
We can determine what we will do with our lives
on the basis of our own desire and ambitions and
our need for recognition and monetary gain; or
we can yield ourselves to the leading of the Holy
Spirit of God who promises to guide us into all
truth (John 16:13).

But how will you know what God wants?
Simply by asking Him. He states very clearly in
His Word that "whatsoever ye shall ask the Father
in my name, he will give it you. Hitherto have

ye asked nothing in my name: ask, and ye shall receive, that your joy may be full" (John 16:23, 24).

James goes a step further when he says, "Ye have not because ye ask not. Ye ask and receive not because ye ask amiss, that ye may consume it upon your lusts" (James 4:2, 3).

We know that if we lack wisdom we can ask God for enlightenment and He will give it liberally, and won't scold us for asking (James 1:5). But we must ask in faith, believing He will give us the answer (James 1:6).

Many of us waste a whole lifetime wishing we had done certain things and are hoping there will yet be time to accomplish what needs to be done. Very few of us are living for today and for what can be done in these moments which are ours for an instant of time. As long as people are human, we will miss God-given opportunities for service. But this is no reason why we should not dedicate our lives to the service of God, whether at home or overseas, whether we're rich or poor, wise or dull, male or female, yellow, red, brown, black, white or striped!

Dedication to the service of God is a happy experience. Paul described what happened to the Macedonian believers when they "first gave their own selves to the Lord": "In a great trial of affliction the abundance of their joy and their deep poverty abounded unto the riches of their liberality. For to their power, I bear record; yea, and beyond their power they were willing of themselves" (2 Cor. 8:2, 3). In the Living Bible it is made much clearer, "They have mixed their wonderful joy with their deep poverty, and the result has been an overflow of giving to others. They gave not only what they could afford, but far more; and I can testify that they did it because they wanted to, and not because of nagging on my part." And Paul's further word concerning them, "Best of all, they went beyond our highest hopes, for their first action was to dedicate themselves to the Lord and to us, for whatever directions God might give to them through us" (2 Cor. 8:5). And these were common, ordinary, garden-type Christians who willingly gave themselves to "full-time service" in a dedication to the Lord which was a blessing to Paul.

So let us dedicate ourselves to God, to be used of Him in whatever way He chooses. But let us be careful that we give Him a fair opportunity to show us *His* will for our lives. The temptation is exceedingly strong to follow our own wisdom and leading. If He leads to foreign soil, be prepared to follow. If He leads to a ministry in the church at home, be prepared to follow. If He leads to a job in business or industry, be prepared to follow. It is not ours to question the direction in which the Lord points us. Our responsibility is to be faithful in obedience to His leading. He will never make us do anything without equipping us for it. So step out in faith without fear. Follow the light. Never lose sight of Him. You'll never regret your decision. And even though you may not be classified by some as a "full-time Christian worker," may you be one nevertheless!

9

Who Should Give an Invitation
to Dedication?

We have talked about what dedication is, who
it involves, and what can happen after a decision
for full-time Christian service has been made. But
we have not made it clear who should give an
invitation to dedication.

Can't anyone do so? Yes. Haven't we established that the call is universal? Yes. Isn't
it the next logical step after the invitation to salvation? Probably. Then what kind of a big deal is
it *who* gives the invitation?

When I was in Bible school, we were bombarded with the challenge to witness and win souls
to Jesus Christ. Some men stood before us to say
we *must* witness to at least one soul every single
day. Others insisted we should actually bring one
soul into a salvation experience every day of our
lives. These were our teachers—and, I might add,
in most cases were our examples. Many of us felt
that this challenge ought to be pursued. Oh, the
poor, unsuspecting people of Providence, Rhode
Island, and its environs! Who can tell what harm

we did in our eagerness to reach that soul each day. It meant grabbing people by the shoulder, picking them up by the neck or coat lapels, shaking them, angering them, and giving them the gospel. In our zeal, we forgot our reason and senses. I'm sure that poor little old lady, trudging along the sidewalk, with her arms filled with grocery bags, appreciated one of us stopping her to tell her she was lost, dying and on her way to hell, while trying to place a tract in her already full hands. I'm sure the priests and people in the Catholic church on the corner appreciated the fact that gospel bombs (tracts rolled in colored cellophane) were constantly thrown in the open door of the church. And the bus driver, who had a schedule to meet and passengers to transport, surely appreciated the question posed to him by a student as he asked, "Have you found Christ?" The bus driver's attitude was revealed in his answer, "I didn't know he was lost!"

Can *anyone* give a witness for Jesus Christ? If he is born-again, of course he can. But do you not see that there are certain inherent problems with a witness at the wrong time, to the wrong person, in the wrong way in the wrong place? A person who is a witness in a legal case does not, indiscriminately, declare his knowledge to everyone he meets. In fact, in many cases, the witnesses are issued a warning concerning whom they speak to and what they say.

The Lord Jesus told His disciples, "Behold, I send you forth as sheep in the midst of wolves: be ye therefore wise as serpents, and harmless as doves" (Matt. 10:16).

Paul said, "Let your speech be alway with

grace, seasoned with salt, that ye may know how ye ought to answer every man" (Col. 4:6).

We ought to be bold, forthright and positive in our witness, but we need to remember that "it is the Spirit that quickeneth; the flesh profiteth nothing" (John 6:63).

The Spirit of God must be allowed the privilege of dealing with the hearts and lives of men. Even the Lord Jesus Christ spent much time in prayer with the Father, asking guidance and direction. We need to follow in His steps in this regard. Then we need to sow the Word of God. We must understand that the "wicked one" will do all in his power to destroy the ability of the seed to come to fruition. Satan deliberately blinds the hearts and minds of men, grasping away the seed, withering the roots of the young vines, causing the concerns of this world to choke the Word's effectiveness in others. But there are some who will hear the Word and understand, and will produce fruit. It is the responsibility of every Christian to broadcast the seed. But it is up to the Spirit of God to produce the fruit.

Now we come to the next step. The Word has done its work. The individual has responded. He has recognized that he is a branch of the one True Vine which gives him his life. And as he takes his life from the Lord, fruit is produced. At this point we encounter the problem posed by this chapter. Who should pick the fruit?

There are many laborers in the vineyard. They are there for various and sundry reasons. Some are picking fruit for the sole purpose of earning a day's pay. Others have a passion to reap a bumper crop. Some have been transported to the vineyard from far-off places for the one purpose of harvesting the crop as quickly as possible. Tomorrow they will work for another master in another vineyard. Some give little care and concern to the way they pick and handle the fruit, or how much of the vine is damaged as they harvest the crop. Others have little allegiance to the owner of the vineyard, but they have a remarkable concern for the appearance and welfare of the fruit. So they handle it with great care as an end in itself. With such a motley crew in the fields, it is a miracle that so much of the fruit actually appears in the market, relatively fresh, unscathed and nourishing.

This is the situation which exists in the Christian Church today. The fruit hangs on the vine. But there is a diversified harvesting crew—some concerned for the money they'll make; some ignorant of the claims of the Master upon the overall harvest; some seeking statistical status; some who have been transported from far-off places to spend a day or a week to pick as much fruit as possible in the time allotted; some who are gravely concerned with the plight of mankind, but who have little or no desire to please the Lord in meeting the needs of people—those who have reversed God's order of things so that they love man first and God second; those who do harm to the Master in their fruit-gathering.

Perhaps you have never given much thought to the invitation to dedication. Visiting speakers have given such invitations as a matter of form, never requesting permission to do so (and if they ask, permission has been granted without question). Sunday school teachers have invited their children to follow the Lord in dedication. Youth leaders have also. Perhaps the neighborhood Bible teacher has assumed this responsibility. And surely the pastor of the church has given scores of such invitations to his people.

So who *should* be responsible to give the invitation for dedication to full-time service?

My dear dad loves the soil. There is very little he doesn't know about growing things. He owned and operated a gladiola farm for a large portion of his life. But although he loves glads, he has also grown every kind of vegetable, many kinds of fruit, and dozens of different kinds of flowers. Even today, somehow out of the sandy soil of Cape Cod, he has a special talent for making things grow in the tiny parcel of land which is his. We are always amazed to see what is flourishing around the foundation of the house, against the fence, in small, home-made hot beds, on the porch, even in the compost pile made from leaves raked from the lawn.

Conditions for growth are not exceptionally favorable on the Cape due to the poor soil, the nightly visits of a wandering racoon, the salt sea air, high winds and a multitude of birds and insects which seek to hinder the crop from producing to its highest potential. Nevertheless, my dad loves each plant and cares for it with loving concern. He stands with hoe in hand, almost daring a weed to lift its ugly head. He maintains a supply of dust, powders and sprays which he applies with diligence to save the plants from the ravages of leaf-eating critters. He has a good supply of fertilizer, made especially for the soil in which his seeds are planted. He waters the garden when necessary, making sure that the proper amount of moisture is maintained at all times. Many times a day he will go out and walk around his plants to make sure they are thriving. He loses a few, through no fault of his own. But most thrive very well because of his patient, knowledgeable, tender, loving care of them. (I might just add that my mother takes the same pains with her indoor plants with similarly good results.)

What is the outcome of all of this expending of time, energy, money and concern? You would only have to visit my parents' home to see the consequences. The miniature palm in the living room is outgrowing its bucket and at its present pace may require cutting a hole in the ceiling in a couple of years; the African violet plants are in constant and abundant bloom; the Christmas poinsettia has grown a foot and its bracts are still beautiful. The gloxinia has been blooming for three months and still has a few buds to open. And outside are the vine-ripened tomatoes, peppers, peas, beans, cucumbers, squash, melons and pumpkins along with carrots, beets, radishes, swiss chard and onions. Then there are the tulips, pansies, geraniums, sweet peas, sunflowers—oh yes, and the dandelions.

It is the Lord himself who has put life into each seed and plant. Through the process of nature, ordained by God, these plants have grown. They've also required the help of those who cared for the plants—those who watched over them, weeded them, watered them, fed them and in other ways showed love and concern for them.

After putting his heart and soul into the hope of reaping from his efforts, it is with extreme joy that my dad harvests the fruits of his labors. I've been with him at times when he's found a simple cucumber previously hidden under a leaf. He is joyous over his discovery, gently lifts the leaf slightly so that the fruit can receive some necessary sunlight. He checks on it again and again to make sure it isn't lost to sight again. Every fruit discovered is a cause for rejoicing. When people visit, they are invited to tour the garden to see the "fruits"—some ready to be picked, some growing to maturity, some still in the flower to develop later.

When the time comes to pick the vegetables, there are always far more than my mom and dad can consume for their own nourishment. The neighbors benefit. Friends who live at a distance are taken basketsful. All who visit are invited to share in the harvest (and some of us visit often during the garden season)! There is always an abundance for all. But very few are allowed to pick those vegetables and flowers. In fact, this is a privilege given only to the immediate family. Dad is not anxious, at this point, for just anyone to come through, take his fruit, injure his plants, tread on his flowers, or cause the yet-to-be-developed fruit to fall to the ground. He assumes full responsibility for each bean, tomato and liatris plant. Therefore, he is very careful about who picks the fruit. Mom leaves the picking pretty much up to Dad (even though she is capable of doing the job well). From earliest childhood, my brother and I were taught by our parents about gardening. So we are allowed access to the ripened harvest. But strangers are not allowed to reap in my father's garden. They may be given some of the crop after it is harvested, but they do not walk in and out of the garden at will.

Perhaps there is no need to draw an analogy between my dad's garden and the question of who should give an invitation to dedication. I cannot give the names of those who are qualified for that responsibility. I cannot even list the positions of those who should pick the fruit in your church. I only know this: it must be someone who loves to see things grow; who will carefully prepare the soil, plant the seed, water and fertilize that plot of ground, seek to destroy the weeds and harmful influences; who will watch over the tender plants (some will need poles around which to wind; others will need a fence to lean against; others will need protection from the sun); who will know when the fruit is ready to be picked; who will know what the best use will be for each portion of the crop (to be put to immediate use; to be shared with others; to be stored in a dark place; to be preserved for future usefulness); who will take great care in the picking so that neither that which is picked nor that which remains will receive any serious hurt; and who, most important of all, will not allow the fruit to stay on the vine until it is overripe and useless.

Perhaps, then, *you* can decide who should give the invitation to dedication. There are thousands of gardens growing. There are many different growing seasons. There are innumerable types of crops. There are numberless tools with which to work. Each situation is different. Wisdom must be exercised in fruit plucking.

If oranges are going to be made into stock feed, any kind of orange, picked by anyone, in any way, can be used—those not quite ripe, those overripe, those which have fallen to the ground, those which are pitted and scarred, those which have no commerical value, even those whose juice has been squeezed out for other purposes. But if the governor of Florida wants to present a gift of his state's fruit to an international dignitary, you can be sure that the fruit will be hand-picked, cared for and packaged by a trusted individual who can cause the fruit to be the finest possible representative of the foremost orange-producing state in the nation!

Now it's up to *you*! Who can best pick and care for the representatives in your church who will spiritually nourish your neighbors—at home and abroad—in the years ahead? An itinerant preacher? A missionary on furlough? A Sunday school teacher? The Christian Education director? The pastor? Someone else? Have you decided? If so, then *that's* who should give an invitation to dedication. He cannot reap the harvest before it is ready. He cannot lessen the growing time. He cannot control the elements which would seek to destroy rather than build up. He cannot save every plant. But he can pick the fruit as it matures and put it to good use. He can carefully turn over the leaves to look for hidden fruit, and bring it to the light. He can ward off the scavenger birds and other pests which would like to devour the plants in their prime before the harvest is gathered. He is, by far, your best choice.

10

Who's Doing Anything

About Dedication?

Although there seems to have been no program yet designed to benefit directly the child who has walked the aisle, there are innumerable opportunities available for the benefit of teen-agers, especially high school and college-aged youth, and men and women of all ages.

At the 1973 Urbana Missionary Convention, held in Urbana, Illinois, some 14,000 students met together as Christian leaders from the United States and overseas told what is happening in the world of missions. At the close of the convention, some 5,000 students signed decision cards indicating their willingness to serve Christ in missionary work abroad.

Never before had there been such a large response to the call to commitment. The problem was, did these students want help and guidance, and should some sort of program be made available to them to strengthen their decision?

Because the leaders of the conference (Inter-

Varsity Christian Fellowship) felt both of these questions could be answered in the positive, they set out to do something about it. Joining together an Advisory Council and a well-chosen faculty, they laid plans for the first 10-week Summer Institute of International Studies. Not only do these young, willing, dedicated young people become able to focus their commitment to a definite task in a specific country, but they also receive college and/or seminary credit.

Through such a program, it is hoped that hundreds of young people will become better acquainted with Christian missions. In so doing, they will become better equipped in their understanding to make mature and right decisions about doing God's will at home or abroad.

Campus Crusade for Christ has been burdened about the need for dedicated young people to become involved in Christian service. Today they are looking for 100,000 men and women who are willing to give at least two years of their lives to reach out among the 210 countries of the world with the message of Jesus Christ. The Agape Movement, as it is called, needs those who have a college degree, or the equivalent business or professional experience. They will give the necessary training, and then send workers to areas where they have been requested.

Churches are responding to the idea of involving their young people in meaningful ministries. One such program has now become an integral part of the Christian Education program at Wheaton Bible Church in Wheaton, Illinois. Called MOP (missions orientation program), it trains teenagers in a regular Sunday school class arranged specifically for them. But each summer these MOPers are sent to various locations for two-week periods (some longer) to minister in distant churches, DVBS programs, backyard clubs, personal witness and music under the sponsorship and leadership of the youth leader and others who are willing to give themselves to this ministry. The program is fully supported by the church and is financially underwritten by those who have an interest in involving young people in Christian service.

A few years ago, Park Street Church in Boston sent a good contingent of high schoolers to Mexico during the summer. The young people painted, cleaned and literally beautified the compound of one of their church missionaries.

Several churches in New Jersey sent out a call to their memberships not too long ago, asking for men to volunteer their vacation time to go to Central America to help in construction work for missionaries. They spent a month there, and came back enthusiastic about Christian service. At least one fellow was so moved by what he saw that he gave up an excellent job with an airline company to go, with his wife, as a missionary to Surinam.

When trouble arose between what was previously known as East and West Pakistan, and a bloodbath of nationalistic endeavor brought about the birth of Bangladesh, people were left without homes, food or medicine. College kids from the United States volunteered to go out to that hot, wet land to do what they could to provide a sense of normalcy to thousands who needed help. They did a heroic job and received the commendation of the leaders of the newly established nation.

With the famine areas of Africa being made known in countries around the world, young and old alike have volunteered their time and resources to go to Ethiopia, Nigeria, and other adversely affected areas. Twenty students left their studies at Seattle Pacific College to serve a short term in Christian service.

Mission boards are pleased with what short-term summer workers, including high school and college-age kids, have been able to do for them. They are calling for more each year. In almost all of these cases, the young person is required to obtain his own financial backing. Often his home church will underwrite the costs. Many times, however, he must engage in a deputation ministry just as full-time missionaries often do. It is encouraging to note that many of these short-termers have come home, finished their schooling, and are now applying to the same or other missions for full-time service.

Short Terms Abroad, an agency located in Downers Grove, Illinois, publishes an annual listing of job opportunities for young and old alike. Terms of service vary from a few weeks to two years or more. Their booklet, "Opportunities '74," lists over 2,055 personnel needs. These workers are being requested by 163 mission agencies under 134 job titles. They currently need more than 16,000 dedicated workers to fill all the openings available to them.

Summer Bible conferences and Christian camping programs need dedicated young people to serve as counselors and other workers. This is excellent preparation for full-time Christian service, for not only is there the opportunity to take advantage of feeding on the Word of God under the teaching of dedicated men of God, but there is the responsibility and discipline of leading others to Christ and teaching them what the Christian life is all about.

There are many organizations looking for summer workers in the field of Christian Education: DVBS work for a period of two to three months; teaching in outdoor Bible classes (in back yards, on the beach, on porches, in parks); home visitation and church census taking. Musical teams are also much in demand.

Youth group interchange gives a good opportunity for Christian service as young people have an opportunity to present a witness to their peers in another church and situation. Week-end retreats planned by and for young people may use a theme which will enhance the commitment to full-time Christian service. Such events are taking place, with profit, across our country as well as in countries abroad.

Yes, there is something being done about dedication. We are grateful for this. One salient point ought not to be overlooked, however. The home church must not allow the responsibility of training its young people to be foisted upon other groups of people, as interested as those groups may be in helping. Denominational groups may be willing to provide outlets for service. But the home church itself must prepare its dedicated young people to become the witnesses they can be and should be for Jesus Christ. And this preparation must have the help, counsel, participation and cooperation of each dedicated individual along with that of his parents (or close friends in the case of older folks), his teachers, his peers and his pastor. Too many times we find a young person joining a Christian service organization, then getting his parents' approval, and finally letting the church know of his decision. The order has somehow gotten reversed. It would seem that God's plan is to work from the home, through the church to the organization. We do, however, have to take into consideration that many homes do not consist of Christian knowledge, love and understanding. There are churches, too, which leave much to be desired when it comes to doing anything with those who are dedicated. In such cases, God-ordained organizations may well fill the gap in offering the necessary training and experience to willing volunteers.

Thousands of men and women and hundreds of thousands of manhours are being put into the task of doing something about dedication. Now the questions come: Can more be done? By whom? How? And let us not forget that all of this work is for nought if dedicated individuals do not take advantage of it. Let's make it known. Let's stir up some zeal, enthusiasm and faithfulness for it.

Perhaps there are other ways in which something may be done for those who are dedicated. Why not turn names and addresses over to Christian organizations to be placed on their mailing lists (with the permission of those involved)? Why don't writers prepare correspondence courses specifically for use with those who have responded to the call to dedication? Why doesn't some Bible college prepare several courses of programmed instruction for use with various age levels on the entire matter of dedication? Why don't Christian organizations hold an Open House or week-end retreat to interest those who are seeking a place of service? Why can't area conferences be held with the specific purpose of sharing with young people the various Christian activities available to them? Why isn't more being written on the overall subject of dedication? Why aren't dedicated children and young people allowed to have responsibilities within the framework of the church? Why aren't these folks being developed for a leadership role? Why isn't the church more eager to help in the financial matters related to those who want to enter full-time Christian service?

Is it wrong to give undue attention to boys and girls, men and women who walk the aisle of dedication? Yes, it is. It discourages those who truly have not felt called to "full-time Christian service." There is nothing humanly commendable about a dedication service. We are glad when individuals are willing to offer themselves. But God himself says, "Many are called, but few are chosen" (Matt. 22:14). God is going to use any and all who are willing to be used of Him. Many of these may be seated in your church and Sunday school, never having publicly responded to a dedication invitation.

Dedication to full-time service demands a continual renewal of commitment to Jesus Christ—hour by hour and day by day. There should be no boasting attached to this act. The praises and plaudits of people will quench the fires of dedication in a young person more quickly than we realize. Older folks will also back away from the constant limelight. Although everything possible should be done to strengthen the act of dedication, this should not include raising these individuals to the status of being superhuman or semi-god. Those who are doing the most about dedication fully recognize this important fact.

And now that we've heard what has been done, is being done, is going to be done, and could be done, what exactly are *you* doing about dedication?

11

Are You *Honestly* Dedicated?

Bishop Moule once stated, "An honest man is the noblest work of God." We give little time and consideration to such a statement. We assume it is true. We mentally assent to its verity. After all, Christians are honest, so that ends that!

Do you remember Diogenes, whose life is surrounded by a maze of legends? One of the stories told concerning him is that he went about with a lantern, in broad daylight "in search of an honest man."

God says in Psalm 32:2, "Blessed is the man . . . in whose spirit there is *no guile*." Luke 8:15, in speaking of the seed that was sown, tells us that "the good ground" includes those who "in an *honest* and good heart, having heard the word, keep it, and bring forth fruit with patience."

The disciples wanted God's blessing upon their ministry. To help them they required dedicated workers who would distribute food to the needy. Their order was, "Wherefore, brethren, look ye out among you seven men of *honest* report, full of the Holy Ghost and wisdom, whom we may appoint over this business" (Acts 6:3).

Paul, giving various pointers to his fellow believers included, "Provide things *honest* in the sight of all men" (Rom. 12:17), and later went a step further by stating, "Providing for *honest* things, not only in the sight of the Lord, but also in the sight of men" (2 Cor. 8:21). Again he recommended, "Let us walk *honestly,* as in the day" (Rom. 13:13), and "Whatsoever things are . . . *honest* . . . think on these things" (Phil. 4:8).

Peter admonished, "Having your conversation [behavior] *honest* among the Gentiles, that, whereas they speak against you as evildoers, they may by your good works, which they shall behold, glorify God in the day of visitation" (1 Pet. 2:12).

Again Paul entreated the Thessalonians, "That ye may walk *honestly* toward them that are without, and that ye may have lack of nothing" (1 Thess. 4:12).

When Paul wrote to Timothy, he exhorted, " . . . that first of all, supplications, prayers, intercessions, and giving of thanks, be made for all men; for kings and for all that are in authority; that we may lead a quiet and peaceable life in all godliness and *honesty*" (1 Tim. 2:1, 2).

The writer of Hebrews ends his book by saying, "Pray for us: for we trust we have a good conscience, in all things willing to live *honestly*" (Heb. 13:18).

And again Paul says in 2 Corinthians 13:7, "Now I pray to God . . . that ye should do that which is *honest.*"

George Washington in his *Farewell Address* (1796) declared, "Honesty is always the best policy."

Shakespeare in his *Timon of Athens*, Act III, Scene 1, Line 30, wrote, "Every man has his fault and honesty is his." Could it be that honesty can get us into trouble? Can it be that there are people in this world who do not understand that there is a difference between honesty and dishonesty?

In the day in which we live, it is, indeed, difficult to distinguish truth from error and honesty from dishonesty. All are swearing upon the Bible itself, that they are being strictly honest. But there are gaps and loopholes, and erasures and blanks and contradictions in testimonies. All claim to be honest. Some appear to be more honest than others. Some are better able to fool the public than others. But the end result has been that judges and juries alike have been stymied and misled concerning the truth, and we come out with distorted and disjointed stories, all given by men who claim to be honest.

It has come to the point where life is just one big game of "To Tell the Truth." If you have watched this TV program, you know that three people appear before a panel. The host of the show reads an affidavit describing what a certain individual is or does. All three people claim to be that individual. Two are lying; one is the real person involved. It is the duty of the panel to choose the honest man or woman from the trio. It is amazing how difficult it is for the panel to choose and agree upon the honest individual. Why? Because not only are the two imposters well-briefed for their role, but the individual himself must appear to be an imposter. This he does in little ways— stumbling over his name, forgetting momentarily where he lives, shaking his head in agreement when a wrong answer is given, pretending not to have heard a pertinent question, or holding off on an answer by pretending the panel has called on someone else when he knows full well they are speaking to him.

It seems inconceivable that we should have to remind Christians of the need for honesty in life and lip. Unfortunately, constant reminders are indicated. We are not, at this time, writing an essay on honesty. We shall, therefore, limit our discussion to some of the facts concerning how it may well affect the act of dedication to full-time Christian service.

First of all, let's consider the individual. When the call was given for dedication, was it made perfectly clear what would be involved? Let's assume it was. The individual felt a tug at his heart-strings. But why did he go forward? Because of his love for his Lord? Because it seemed to be expected of him? Because he was a leader? Because a friend responded? Because his dad was the preacher? Because he felt pressured into it? Because his parents urged him? Because Christian workers "run in his family"? Because "it was the thing to do"? Did he honestly go forward in full commitment to Jesus Christ because he truly felt the call of God upon his life for full-time Christian service? Did he honestly feel as Paul did when he said, "For necessity is laid upon me; yea, woe is unto me, if I preach not the gospel!"? (Note that Paul prefixes this statement with an honest appraisal, namely, "For though I preach the gospel, I have nothing to glory of," 1 Cor. 9:16.)

Only God can see into the heart of an individual to discover his thoughts and intents. Only God can choose those whom He calls. Only God, the Holy

Spirit, can seal the dedication which has been made. Only God can consecrate that which has been dedicated. God alone knows if this was a spontaneous, emotional, rational, or plausible commitment. But remember, the individual, too, ought to be aware of the depth of his dedication. He it is who has made that "aisle walk" with God. True, he may not know where this first step may lead, but he is willing for it and in all honesty gives himself to the prospect of full-time Christian service. He should have an answer for any who might ask why he went forward. He should be assured that he responded to God's invitation "to go" and not just to man's invitation "to come."

And suppose an individual goes forward at the call for dedication and later discovers he is not interested in, qualified for, or called to what many call "full-time" service. Must he become a minister or a missionary just the same? Must he live a life of regret if he follows another path in a different profession? It is a pitiful thing that far too many Christians have done just that.

But let's be reasonable—and I think we can assume that God is, too. Have you ever heard a four-year-old say, "I'm going to be a nurse when I grow up"? She tells her mother and dad, and with all honesty she believes, and they believe that she will be a nurse. At seven, however, she comes under the influence of a talented music teacher, and at ten she decides to be a professional pianist. Then at fourteen, she comes into a new and living relationship with God through Jesus Christ and a year later dedicates her life for full-time Christian service. She is sincerely honest, and to the best of her knowledge, she will become a missionary.

After her first year at Bible college, she meets a fine Christian fellow who teaches Sunday school in the church where she has been assigned to lead the youth group. They date, fall in love, talk of marriage, but alas, she confesses, "I can't marry you. I promised God I'd be a missionary and you don't feel called."

So giving back his ring, shedding buckets of tears, and determining to go to the field, she finally makes it. She has trouble learning the language, is sick more than well, and is all too often lonely. After 3-4 years, she has been sent home, her health ruined, unable to return to the field. Her fiance has now married. Now what of God's call upon her life? Why did she go to the field? Honestly now? What do you think her answer was? Did the same God who called her out call her home again? This is entirely possible. Did God really intend for her to marry that young fellow and serve Him at home? This, too, is possible. In trying not to turn back, having put her hand to the plow, she had become a "foreign" missionary—only to seemingly have to turn back anyway. What is the answer to such questions?

We seem to enjoy making life difficult—far more difficult than God intended for it to be. You see, God created us with a free will—a device to help us choose and decide the issues of life with which we are faced. We are not robots. We live and move and have our being in the freedom of our own choices. This is part of God's abundant grace and love on our behalf.

Somehow, through the passing of time, we have come to set up choices, limits, standards and strategies which being interpreted by "evangelical" Christians mean, "You can serve God only if," or "If you've dedicated your life to God you must," or "If you've once determined to serve the Lord in a particular way, you cannot change your mind," etc.

But let's go back a bit and suppose that our little girl who wanted to be a nurse at four decides to be an architect at twenty-four. She is a Christian. This is the sixth time she's decided on what her life's work will be. But she never walked the aisle at the call for dedication. Be honest now. Does it matter what she does as long as she does it "heartily as unto the Lord"? (Col. 3:23). Could it be possible that she had determined to serve Christ, though she had never walked the aisle? Only she and God know that, of course. But why is it she can change her mind six times quite unobtrusively and acceptably while those who are "dedicated" are put in an immovable concrete mold (which may or may not honor God)?

Is it possible for an individual to state, "I made a mistake," or "I really didn't understand," or "I didn't give it enough thought," or "I'm truly unhappy continuing in this direction"? Of course it is. And in all honesty, if he feels that way, he should seek the Lord's will in another direction. Some people seem to have the idea that God's will almost always is burdensome, unpalatable, self-sacrificing and financially disintegrating, and they force others to assume these views. (These people are easy to find. Just have a missionary say he needs a refrigerator, Jeep or dishwasher to take back to the field with him. You'll find out who those people are!)

But let's not forget the other side of the cloth. The individual must bear some responsibility and follow-through in the matter of Christian service.

He must honestly face the issue. He must not change his mind as the mood suits. He must earnestly rely upon God's Word and the Spirit to show him God's will for his life. He must not assume that dedication can be an off-again, on-again type of experience. He must be sure that his motives are pure, his reasoning apt and his direction clear. Honesty with God, with himself, and with others is a priority concern. Let there be no substitute for that.

We must also take into consideration how the honesty, or lack of it, on the part of parents can affect the dedication to full-time Christian service.

How many parents have told their children, "Even before you were born, we dedicated you to the Lord!" Or they may have a certificate signed by Pastor Smith indicating that on the third of May, in the year such and so, Jim was dedicated to the Lord at the age of three months. To them this has always meant that their son would one day be a minister. And when he decides to become a professional football player, there is the deepest disappointment on the part of the parents. If they were honest, they would acknowledge the fact that being a minister was *their* idea of God's will for Jim. It was at *their* urging and insistence that he had gone forward to volunteer for full-time service *IF* God should direct. But God didn't direct him that way, and his parents are sure he has missed God's best. Even the fact that he is the best fullback in the profession, and is known and spoken of highly for his Christian testimony and sense of fair play cannot assuage the grief of his parents because he is not a minister, and therefore not in full-time service.

How many parents have tried to force their

youngsters into "Christian work" by telling them, "When you were three, you told us you wanted to be a missionary." The child has no recollection whatsoever of this event. But his parents are holding him to it, nevertheless.

On the other hand, there is a different side of honesty which must be faced. This has to do with young people who dedicate themselves to the Lord for service, but are thwarted in their attempts to fulfill their commitment by parents who are quite willing for them to be a pastor or Christian Education director at home, but who are absolutely petrified at the thought of their children serving at an isolated overseas post. Some are so protective that they won't so much as allow their children to conduct a Daily Vacation Bible School in a ghetto, work at the local Coffee House, or play the piano at the Rescue Mission. Let's be honest. This is true in case after case.

Parents have a responsibility to their children, but there comes a time in the life of each child when he must choose for himself. The mother eagle protects her young at all costs, but there comes a day when she gently pushes them out of their comfortable nest on the side of the cliff. You can be sure they learn to fly in a hurry!

Parents can overprotect and stifle the dedication of their children. Can they be honest in dedicating their children to God and then disallow them to pursue God's will for their lives? Oh, we have *so* much to learn in this area of honesty—and we're such dreadfully slow learners!

The church must also share in the honesty of dedication. It is not their prerogative to give dedication invitation upon dedication invitation with no explanation of what it means and no follow-through after it happens. Statistics look good on the annual report, but make sure they are honest figures. I know of at least one organization which came out with astounding statistics year by year. They worked in almost every state, and at one time were allowed to hold Bible classes in the public schools. A worker in a small town might teach a total of 200 children through schools and home classes during a week. At the end of the year his report would state that he reached 7500 children that year. How? Well, for nine months of the year he reached 200 children a week. It was a simple matter of multiplication (plus some adding for the summer months). True, there were only 200 *different* children involved, but who would stop to figure that out? The number 7500 was far more impressive. You can imagine what the figures looked like for large cities!

And churches, especially those who have altar calls regularly, will find certain individuals going forward at every call. Nevertheless, these go into the annual report as separate and individual decisions. You see how deceiving it could be if one person went forward every week. Why, at the end of the year in the column for response to call for dedication, the number 52 could be listed. It, of course, would be embarrassing if the district superintendent, bishop, or president of the convention were to drop in and ask, "Where are they?" and the church had to reply, "He's right over there!"

Sometimes the invitation itself is deceptive. First a call for commitment to God, then the raising of the hand, then the request to come forward, then prayer with a member of the congregation and counsel in the room to the left of the platform. By the time the individual has gotten "dedicated," he's been committed to something far different than was specified when he raised his hand, or when he walked down the aisle.

The church can be dishonest in praying for its young people to commit themselves to full-time service. It is far easier to pray, "Lord, here am I. Send young John," than to pray that God will show every member of the church what He would have him/her to do.

The church can also pretend to have a keen interest in obtaining a response from its young people, and yet negate what it says by lack of any action following the service of dedication.

How honest is a church which gives an opportunity for dedication, but is unwilling to assume prayerful and financial support of those who respond?

And how honest are older folks when they are faced with the responsibility and privilege of full-time Christian service? How many excuses do they make for denying the Lord's call? Who comes first in their lives? What holds them back?

Let's take a long look at this whole matter. Although we are Christians, are we truly honest?

We don't hear much about some of Jesus' disciples. One of those was Nathaniel. But Jesus paid him an outstanding compliment upon their first face-to-face meeting. You'll remember that Philip told Nathaniel that he had found Jesus about whom Moses and the prophets had spoken. Nathaniel was not ecstatic, emotional or enthused. His honest question, openly expressed, was, "Can there any good thing come out of Nazareth?" And Philip simply replied, "Come and see for yourself." And as Nathaniel approached Jesus, he heard Him say, "Behold an Israelite indeed, in whom is no guile" (John 1:45-47). What a compliment! Jesus knew Nathaniel was frank, candid and honest. He was not given to craftiness, cunning or trickery. He was what he was and who he was, and Jesus appreciated that.

A magazine reported a remark made by Allen Kissinger (Henry's brother) upon successfully buying into a Japanese company. Very few Americans have been able to accomplish this feat. The crux of the matter? "Trust!" Mr. Kissinger is reported to have stated. "You cannot do business with the Japanese without a commitment of the spirit—a commitment in terms of integrity, vision, a belief in the reliability of partners. Very few U.S. companies recognize this need for total commitment." (*Newsweek*, April 1, 1974, p. 62)

Do you see what we're trying to say? You cannot do business with God without a total commitment of the spirit—in terms of honesty, vision, and a trust in the utter reliability of a faithful God.

In this regard, may I ask something? Are you *honestly* dedicated? Do you allow for honest dedications? God looks for, expects and appreciates honesty in *all* His people. Don't disappoint Him!

12

Dedication, Discipleship and Destination

Throughout the pages of this book, we have sought to determine the meaning, methods, problems and outcomes of the act of dedicating one's life to full-time Christian service. It can be and, indeed, ought to be a very meaningful experience based on love and obedience to the claims of God upon one's life. It was Paul who said, "I am debtor both to the Greeks, and to the Barbarians; both to the wise, and to the unwise" (Rom. 1:14). Because the gospel of Christ had come to him and he had been made a new creature in Christ, he owed something to the world of which he was a part.

If we are in financial debt, there are at least three ways to get around it: (1) We can attempt to meet our obligations; (2) we can declare bankruptcy, or (3) we can skip the country. With a shrewd lawyer, there are other ways of avoiding the issue, or circumventing it.

There are also at least three ways to cope with our spiritual debt: (1) We can seek to find and do the will of God; (2) we can make it known that we just do not have the time, talent, ability, patience, desire, etc., to do God's will—we are, as it were, spiritually bankrupt; or (3) we can "duck out" on our obligations by removing ourselves from the forces which would cause our consciences to bear the consequences of our failure to meet our spiritual debts. By using excuses, by exercising shrewd thinking, by manipulating circumstances, and in many other ways we may be able to avoid or circumvent the issue of dedication.

But we ought not to think of dedication as a negative act—something which must be done in order to appease God and our fellow Christians.

If dedication does not and cannot come from a willing mind and a cheerful heart, then it is doubtful that the individual is acting maturely or that he is motivated of God. Whether he is six or sixty makes no difference. It is the heart attitude which matters. And if doing God's will is a hard chore and exists apart from joy in its doing, it is doubtful that it is truly God's will in which you are engaged. If there is assurance of the will of God, then it is imperative that the individual should search his heart to discover his true attitude toward it. There may be something in the life withholding the blessing of God. If so, God will shut off the power until all the lines are repaired and communication is restored.

Dedication is important, but perhaps we have tried to put too much emphasis upon the specific act of that aisle walk with God. Not all of us came into a right relationship with God through Jesus Christ in exactly the same way. God deals individually with the souls of men. The Holy Spirit draws those who are His. And man cannot—I repeat, CANNOT—dictate to God what He can do, to whom He can do it, and how He must act in a given situation. We are guilty of this, to be sure.

We are not good judges of how God is working in the lives of His people. Perhaps all of us would be better off if we were to dedicate our lives to Him in such a way that our thoughts, criticisms, words and actions could be used for the building up of the body of Christ rather than for the demolition of it.

I was reminded of this recently as spring unfolded in my native New England. The crocuses, jonquils, iris, rhododendron, lilacs, tulips, dogwood, forsythia and apple trees were in full bloom. The willows, birches, maples—even the oaks had developed their full greenery. As I looked out my dining room window, I watched a giant tree in a neighboring yard. It towered high above the two-story home there. Yet there was no sign of a bud or a leaf on the tree. One day I remarked to a friend, "I wonder why the yardmen haven't come to cut down that huge dead tree in the next yard? If a storm or high wind should develop, it could be extremely dangerous to all of us."

Then it rained for two days, followed by a rise in temperature. On the second day of 80° readings, I couldn't believe my eyes. That "dead" tree was completely garmented in large green leaves. I still don't know where they came from. But I learned a lesson. Too many times we look at a life and decide there is little use for it, so with our criticism and "Christian" concern, we decide the only good that could ever come from it is to chop it down and at least use it for firewood.

God looks at things in a different way than we do! He knew there was life in that "dead" tree. He knows the potential of every individual.

And He is in no hurry to blot anyone off His list. Sometimes He works in silence or quietness. Sometimes He works in loud thunderings. But He can and does know those who are dedicated to Him. It is good when individuals acknowledge their dedication before the corporate church, if the church can be encouraged to back them in their decision and to give help whenever and wherever possible. This should be the normal pattern. Unfortunately, it is not. It is time for the church to become debtor to those who respond to the dedication invitation. Again, we have been guilty with "too little and too late."

There is more to the matter of serving God than a dedication to full-time Christian service. Such dedication, at best, includes a very, very small percentage of the total Christian population of the world. (And let us never forget that dedication to full-time service is not a specialty reserved for American Christians. Africans, Indians, Italians, Ecuadoreans, Islanders, Japanese—Christians from all over the world—are responding to the call to "go . . . preach . . . teach . . . baptize." We often tend to overlook the fact that anyone is doing anything for the sake of the gospel apart from those born in the United States!)

The Lord Jesus Christ did not put undue emphasis upon dedication. But His entire ministry focused on discipleship. In fact, His emphasis in the Great Commission is, "Go ye and make disciples of all nations." He was our example in this as He chose disciples throughout His earthly ministry.

What *is* a disciple? Again we go to Webster's Dictionary. He says a disciple is "one who receives instruction from another: one who accepts the doctrines of another and assists in spreading or implementing them; a professed follower of Christ; a convinced adherent of a particular school." It also can mean to teach or to train. It bears a resemblance to "being disciplined or instructed or teachable."

Although we think of only twelve men in reference to the disciples of Jesus, the Scriptures use the word to describe followers of Jesus apart from and other than those chosen few. Those who were later called Christians (first at Antioch) were those who were formerly referred to as disciples.

If this is true, are we not, then, disciples? We certainly ought to be—every last born-again Christian upon the face of the earth. If we are not disciples, then Christianity is a failure, since God's purpose for His people through the ages has been "to make disciples." Either others have failed in their efforts to bring us to discipleship, or we have failed in our response to their teaching.

What does discipleship involve? Jesus made it very clear. He maintained that if something is worth much, it also costs much. (And He spoke from personal experience.) Jesus said, "If any man come to me, and hate not his father, and mother, and wife, and children, and brethren, and sisters, yea, and his own life also, he cannot be my disciple. And whosoever doth not bear his cross, and come after me, cannot be my disciple" (Luke 14:26, 27). Again He stated, "Whosoever he be of you that forsaketh not all that he hath, he cannot be my disciple" (Luke 14:33).

What do disciples do? Again, Jesus gives us the pattern: "And his disciples believed on him"

(John 2:11). "If ye continue in my word, then are ye my disciples indeed; and ye shall know the truth, and the truth shall make you free" (John 8:31). "Herein is my Father glorified, that ye bear much fruit; so shall ye be my disciples" (John 15:8). "The disciple is not above his master: but every one that is perfect shall be as his master" (Luke 6:40).

Already we note, then, (1) that disciples believe on the Lord Jesus Christ; (2) that disciples dwell in and live out the teachings of the Word of God; (3) that disciples reproduce themselves; and (4) disciples are in subjection to God as sons, and share all the privileges and responsibilities as members of the family of God.

Is discipleship a drag? It *shouldn't* be! It ought to be the experience of every follower of Jesus to join with those who lined His pathway as He rode triumphantly into the city of Jerusalem. Luke says, "The whole multitude of the disciples began to rejoice and praise God with a loud voice for all the mighty works that they had seen; saying, Blessed be the King that cometh in the name of the Lord: peace in heaven, and glory in the highest" (Luke 19:37, 38).

Does discipleship carry special privileges? Indeed it does. It is the sheep that follows the shepherd most closely which receives the best fruit. Mark 4:34 tells us, "And when they were alone, he expounded all things to his disciples." What a choice privilege—to be taught the truth by the One who *is* the truth.

But do those special privileges place the followers of Jesus on a pedestal? Not at all. Jesus tried to clarify this point when He set an example and exhorted His disciples to follow in His steps. "He began to wash the disciples' feet, and to wipe them with the towel wherewith he was girded. . . . So after he had washed their feet, and had taken his garments, and was set down again, he said unto them, Know ye what I have done to you? Ye call me Master and Lord: and ye say well; for so I am. If I then, your Lord and Master, have washed your feet, ye also ought to wash one another's feet" (John 13:5, 12-14). This is difficult discipline for the disciple—but a necessary one.

Is discipleship easy? Most of us consider it extremely difficult. Apparently we forget something of consequence along its pathway which *makes* it difficult. Perhaps it is because we try rather than trust. Jesus said, "Come . . . take my yoke upon you . . . learn of me . . . find rest . . . for my yoke is *easy*, and my burden is light" (Matt. 11:28-30).

Does discipleship involve more than just saying we believe in Christ and we want to follow Him? Yes, it does. Far more. Do you remember when Jesus told His disciples what lay in store for Him through death, burial and resurrection? He also told Peter, "This night, before the cock crow, thou shalt deny me thrice" (Matt. 26:34). Peter couldn't believe what he was hearing. You see, he didn't know himself nearly as well as Jesus knew him! So Peter said, "Though I should die with thee, yet will I not deny thee. Likewise also said *all* the disciples" (Matt. 26:35).

An old proverb says, "Talk is cheap." It costs nothing to open your mouth and speak. Standing behind and following through on what you say, however, can be very costly. This is clearly shown in Scripture when we read that when Jesus was betrayed and taken off for trial, "all the disciples forsook him, and fled" (Matt. 26:56). Peter followed afar off (Matt. 26:58) and when he was recognized, he vehemently denied that he ever knew Jesus.

After the disciples failed their Lord, did He cut them off and forget them? Not at all. When the women appeared at the empty tomb, the angel said to them, "Go quickly, and tell his disciples that he is risen from the dead" (Matt. 28:7). And when the disciples met with Jesus, "they worshipped him: but some doubted" (Matt. 28:16, 17). Did the Lord give up then? No. He still had confidence in them. So much so, in fact, that He gave them an overwhelmingly tremendous commission which He fully expected them to carry out. "And Jesus came and spake unto them, saying, All power is given unto me in heaven and in earth. Go ye therefore, and teach all nations, baptizing them in the name of the Father, and of the Son, and of the Holy Ghost: teaching them to observe all things whatsoever I have commanded you: and, lo, I am with you always, even unto the end of the world" (Matt. 28:18-20). Go and make disciples! Even though the disciples doubted Jesus—and had earlier denied Him—He was willing to use them. They were the best He had. If He was disappointed in them, He never confessed to it. His confidence was rewarded, of course, as we read of what they accomplished for Him following His resurrection. To help them in their discipleship, Jesus sent the Holy Spirit to indwell His followers. Most of us, I fear, would have long since chopped down the "dead" tree!

Are there distinguishing characteristics about discipleship? Surely there ought to be. It is to our shame that we, as followers of Jesus Christ, are not easily recognizable in the world today. There are many marks of a true disciple. We have already mentioned some of these when we asked, "What do disciples do?" But the Lord always makes things as simple as possible, and He tells us the one thing that sets us apart as His followers: *"By this shall all men know that ye are my disciples, if ye have love one to another"* (John 13:35).

If Jesus Christ is not our Lord, we cannot be His disciples. Discipleship demands discipline. It involves self-denial and cross-bearing; renouncing all that would hinder the fulfillment of God's highest and best for our lives; leaving behind anyone or anything that comes before our commitment to Jesus Christ; continuing to walk by faith, according to the expressed commands of the Word of God; leading others into an awareness of their spiritual need and directing them into discipleship. And all of our doing, saying, and being must be carried out in love.

Long years have passed since my days as a missionary in a foreign land. There has been time to consider that commitment. And in considering, I have found a basic lack in my service. I did not go forth to disciple. I went out to scatter seed upon hard, dry, desert soil. The seed did not take root. I wouldn't trade those days of ministry for any other experience in my life—but they were not fruitful in a harvest of souls for the Lord. In looking back, I believe the experience was necessary to bring *me* into a position of discipleship. But I failed to bring others into that kind of relationship with the Lord. I was dedicated. But dedication is not enough.

Our destination is determined by the extent of our dedication and the depth of our discipleship. This does not mean that those who go farthest away, geographically, from the place where they started are the most dedicated and favored disciples. Distance has no bearing, whatsoever, on the commitment of God's servants.

Are you acquainted with the greatest Missionary of all time? Have you followed Him as He went from place to place discipling? Where was His first ministry? In the town of Cana, at a wedding. What an unlikely place to disciple! Everyone's attention was upon the wedding party and the reception. And how far from home was He? All of about five miles! Shouldn't He have been off in Asia Minor somewhere? Apparently not! As a matter of fact, Jesus never went to the "uttermost part of the earth" in the sense that we tend to interpret His commission, although He did go to "Jerusalem, and all Judea, and Samaria." Perhaps His coming from heaven to earth would suffice for "all the world." Or did He leave that for His disciples to do? His only comment, in His prayer to the Father (John 17:18), was, "As thou hast sent me into the world, even so have I also sent them into the world." He gave many invitations to salvation. He gave many invitations for discipleship. There is, however, no invitation to dedication spoken of during our Lord's earthly ministry, as we understand it to be the dedication of one's life to full-time Christian service.

Although no special service of dedication is mentioned, there had to be a time of dedication

in the life of each individual who came to Jesus
for service. It was a moment of "forgetting those
things which are behind" (whether it be fishing,
tax collecting, or whatever)—a moment of commitment to Him with all it would involve. Once
this point was established, Jesus provided them
with some follow-through. He taught them. He
showed them a needy world. He sent them forth.
He prayed for them. He communicated with them.
He helped them when the job was more than they
could handle. He even went with them on many
of their missions and they went with Him on His.
It is small wonder, then, that dedication was followed by discipleship. This is where we seem to
have gone astray in the day in which we live.
Dedication has been considered a solitary act
which will meet the criteria set down by our Lord
when He called us by His grace. No! Dedication
is of little benefit of and by itself. Yet, the Christian
Church has allowed it to become an extremely
important entity. Once it has been accomplished,
we have left our dedicated people to work out their
own dedication—*sans* the help of the church or
anyone in it.

If, on the other hand, we could establish these
willing volunteers as disciples, we would solve
many of our problems and theirs, as they seek
to do the will of God. Being a disciple is a full-time
job. But we must remember that the field is the
world. We can be a witness at the weddings in
our neighborhoods as well as preaching the gospel
in the churches, the jungles and the far-flung corners of the earth.

Perhaps we need to rethink our understanding
of "full-time Christian service." You may not come

up with anything different than you've believed throughout your Christian experience. Then again, as you consider dedication, discipleship and destination, you may come up with an entirely new and better concept which will use to the full all that is being offered in the service of God by those who walk the aisle with Him. Or you may even decide to give an invitation for discipleship rather than for dedication. To date we have seen too many dedications and too few disciples. On the other hand, we need to encourage far more dedications from among the disciples.

13

How Much Does Dedication Cost?

There is a familiar adage which aptly describes most of life: "You get what you pay for!" In an economy which lingers at the brink of disaster, we may question the validity of such a statement. Yet, even though prices and wages are in a constant state of flux, it is still fairly basic that "you get what you pay for."

When we speak of the cost of dedication, we are not, in fact, dealing primarily with finances. Let's take this into another realm. How much does it cost when you buy a tin of tuna fish for your cat? At current prices, it ranges from 15¢ to 30¢ for a 6 oz. can. But beyond this obvious and fairly nominal cost, there is a far greater price involved. First of all, the tuna had to be killed. In preparation for that event, scores of years of time, energy and intelligent workmen were spent in discerning where the best tuna fishing is, and in designing boats and equipment to facilitate the capture of these fish. It took many others, in every part of the world, to determine the best use of every part of the fish after it was caught. Then men and women were assigned the job of cutting, canning, labelling, packaging and shipping the finished product to the super market. The transportation industry got into the act. Then it was up to the market owner or manager to make a place for the tuna on his shelves, advertise it, make displays to promote it and hire workmen to collect the cost of each tin sold. It also involves someone who must purchase it, take it home, open it, place it in a dish and get the cat to eat it (which in many instances is the most difficult thing to accomplish). Many other steps, too numerous to mention, are involved in the cost of one tin of tuna.

Who can tell the cost of a tin of tuna? We could never list the names of those who have had a part in the finished product. We can only assume what the loss of that tuna did to the balance of nature, and how many other tuna could have been given life if he had not died.

Of course, in all of the steps in getting a tuna from ocean to cat, there is the matter of finances to be considered.

Unfortunately, all too often Christians deserve Paul's warning as he said, "The love of money is the root of all evil" (1 Tim. 6:10). It was his understanding that "we brought nothing into this world, and it is certain we can carry nothing out. And having food and raiment let us be therewith content" (1 Tim. 6:7, 8).

Yet, Christians hold their pursestrings with an iron fist. They are perfectly willing to give up almost every comfort, pleasure and material benefit. But their money is their own. Even a tithe is far too much to give to God. Can you imagine what could be done to advance the gospel of Christ if every born-again Christian gave a tenth of his money to the work of God? (And *every* Christian includes pastors, missionaries, Christian workers—and children.) There is little one can do with money. You can save it, spend it or give it away. True, it can buy *things,* but even then, it can only purchase that which will perish. It can never buy true love, truth, honor, happiness, humility, friendship and the things that really count for eternity.

We are afraid of riches; we're more afraid of poverty. Yet God is no respecter of persons (Rom. 2:11). He provides for all our needs. David once declared, "I have been young, and now am old; yet have I not seen the righteous forsaken, nor his seed begging bread" (Ps. 37:25). Paul told the Ephesians that "he [God] is able to do exceeding abundantly above all that we ask or think" (Eph. 3:20).

God intends for us to dedicate our finances to Him. It *does* cost money. But oh, the rewards! Jesus gave us a formula which truly works. I don't know how it works, but I have proven it, and seen it proven by others, over and over again. He said, "Give, and it shall be given you; good measure, pressed down, and shaken together, and running over, shall men give into your bosom. For with the same measure that ye mete withal it shall be measured to you again" (Luke 6:38).

Even Solomon, in his human reasoning, was able to say, "Cast thy bread upon the waters: for thou shalt find it after many days" (Eccle. 11:1).

There is at least one mention in the Scriptures concerning God's feelings involved in the act of dedication where it deals with money. You remember the story from the book of Acts. The believers at Jerusalem "were of one heart and of one soul: neither said any of them that ought of the things which he possessed was his own; but they had all things common" (Acts 4:32). "Neither was there any among them that lacked" (Acts 4:34). Those who had land or possessions sold them, and gave the proceeds to the apostles and distribution was made according to the needs of each man.

But just like modern-day believers, Ananias and Sapphira (Acts 5), when they sold a possession, determined that they could logically deduct the tax, the broker's fee, the Social Security, etc. So they ended up giving God only a part of that which was dedicated to Him. The Scripture states very clearly that the possession had been theirs, and even when they sold it, the money belonged to them. So far there seems to be no problem. But there is, you see, for they had dedicated themselves and all they had unto the Lord. Thus, when they gave the apostles only a part of that which they had promised God, they were told that they had lied against the Holy Ghost, and because they lied to God, they were struck dead—both of them. God was not nearly so concerned about the financial aspects of the problem as He was about the heart attitude of those who were dedicated.

This is the seriousness with which God looks at dedication. Does it cost? Of course it does. Does God hold us to our commitment? Indeed He does—if it is made with a full knowledge of what it involves.

Sometimes dedication involves living for Jesus Christ. Other times it involves dying for Him. We all know of those who have been given a death sentence through their dedication. The Lord Jesus himself was involved in this. We have only to read Hebrews 11 to learn that there have been those through every generation who have given their lives because of their dedication to Him. Stephen gave his life, was the first martyr of the church, and received the honor of seeing Christ stand to meet him (see Acts 7:56). Read Fox's *Book of Martyrs* if you want to see what dedication cost thousands of Christians. In our own lifetime we remember well what dedication cost Jim Elliot, Nate Saint, Pete Fleming, Ed McCully and Roger Youderian as they gave their lives on a desolate beach among the Auca Indians. The late Dr. V. Raymond Edman believed that their martyrdom proved conclusively that first-century devotion to Christ is still alive.

We have heard of martyrs in many countries of the world. There are also many whose names we may never hear during our earthly sojourn, including thousands upon thousands who have been willing to suffer and die in countries far removed from America—many Chinese, Africans, Indians, Afghans, Brazilians, Russians . . . Yes, dedication can cost one his life.

But does everyone commit himself to death as he walks the aisle with God? Physical death? No! (Although he ought to be willing even for this.) Death to self? Yes! (Gal. 2:20). And I do not mean to take anything away from the martyrs through the ages—nor could I, for they, too, first faced this type of death . . . but living for God is sometimes more difficult than dying for Him. I do not know what it would have been like to sit around a table at Shell Mera, Ecuador, and hear the detailed report of how my husband had been cruelly murdered by those whom he had hoped to bring to salvation through faith in Jesus Christ. I think, even in that moment of numbness, I would have welcomed dying for Him rather than having to pick up the pieces and continue in dedication to the will of God while the whole world watched. Yet God reminds us, "For my thoughts are not your thoughts, neither are your ways my ways, saith the Lord. For as the heavens are higher than the earth, so are my ways higher than your ways, and my thoughts than your thoughts" (Isa. 55:8, 9). And as we dedicate our lives to Him, He assures us that "no weapon that is formed against thee shall prosper; and every tongue that shall rise against thee in judgment thou shalt condemn. This is the heritage of the servants of the Lord, and their righteousness is of me, saith the Lord" (Isa. 54:17).

We note two things of interest here: (1) we are servants, and (2) we are clothed in *His* righteousness. Therefore we see that dedication costs us our cause for boasting. To *God* be the glory. Great things *He* hath done!

Dedication costs us in the matter of time. We cannot afford to put off our service for the Master. Paul contends that "the time is short" (1 Cor. 7:29). He also advises us that we should be "redeeming the time" (Col. 4:5). John indicates ever greater urgency as he states that "the time is at hand" (Rev. 1:3).

As workers together with Him, we must keep in mind that "now is the accepted time; behold, now is the day of salvation" (2 Cor. 6:2). It is essential that we go to work in the vineyard as early as possible, for "the night cometh, when no man can work" (John 9:4). It is impossible to hoard time. All you have is what you spend. Again, "you get what you pay for."

The Communists make no bones about what dedication means to them. Strictly and concisely it involves: absolute acceptance, absolute discipline, absolute dedication and absolute action. That's quite clear, wouldn't you say?

But what of those who walk the aisle with God to dedicate their lives to full-time Christian service? Is there a cost involved? There *ought* to be. We've made dedication such a mamby-pamby, indefinite sort of commitment that we have not yet begun to realize its importance and what it involves. You see, it costs all you were, all you are, and all you ever hope to be. It costs all you've had, all you have, and all you ever hope to obtain. It costs all you've said, all you say, and all you ever hope to say.

How many times have you heard that all Christians should go *or* give *or* pray? It was assumed that if you wanted to do one, you were excused or excluded from the others. That is an untruth. There is clear evidence in the Word of God that all are to go *and* give *and* pray. Where you do it is of little concern. How faithful you are in doing it is what really matters.

Perhaps we, in America, have been the slowest learners in this matter of dedication. In Pakistan, we rejoiced when we saw Christians who really dedicated themselves to the work of God and the ministry of the saints. National pastors place their own lives, as well as those of their families, in jeopardy as they give themselves continually and wholeheartedly to the Lord. Christians who have nothing of this world's goods are willing to give their chicken, water buffalo or camel so that God's work can go on and the pastor can be supported. It is never surprising to find such things as beans, a potato, a cup of rice, a stalk of sugar cane or a handful of wheat in the offering plates around the world. These are dedicated and sacrificial gifts. It is of these that Jesus spoke when He saw the widow cast her two mites into the treasury and said, "For all they did cast in of their abundance; but she of her want did cast in all that she had, even all her living" (Mark 12:44).

Have we ever taken time to count the cost of dedication? Or do we consider dedication as something we skim off the top or drain from the bottom, leaving the bulk of the best to our own devices and desires?

"You get what you pay for." Could this be the reason why Christianity is not keeping pace with world growth? Why denominations are cutting back on the number of missionaries they're able to send out? Why church membership itself in many sectors is dropping in the U.S.? We aren't paying enough!

Not too long ago we "concluded" the longest "war" in American history. It cost billions of U.S. dollars, tens of thousands of U.S. lives and a cleavage in confidence concerning U.S. leadership in this struggle. The "war" will never come to a halt under present circumstances. You see, the U.S., although it felt an obligation to become involved in the matter, has never been dedicated to the destruction or overthrow of "evil" and the reinforcement of "good." If we had been motivated by such dedication, the "war" could have been won in a very short time, with the loss of far fewer men, and with far greater possibilities of a cease-fire or temporary peace in that area of the world. But our commitment was only token dedication, not all out dedication. And we see we have not really won!

How many Christians have paid many times the cost of dedication, to further their own ends and raise their own status? It all depends on how you look at dedication. What do you want to achieve? What is your motivation? How much are you willing to put into it? How much do you want to win the victory?

Carefully consider each of these questions. They are the clue to how much dedication costs.

And for those of us who are considered to be members of "the establishment," it might be well for us to look at our young people today to see what they expect dedication to involve. In finances alone, they put most of us to shame. At Urbana '73 for example, the cash offering for missions at just one evening service totaled over $150,000. At Park Street Church Missionary Conference in 1974, 277 high school youngsters pledged over $37,000 to the missions program of the church while the Grad Group pledged over $67,000. And all these fellows and girls are still in school. Yet they have dedicated their money to full-time Christian service, willing to go without many of the "niceties" of life in order to fulfill their commitment. (Please remember that when you see a young person who owns but two sets of blue jeans, and operates as his own barber!)

Thousands of young people have offered their lives for service during this past year. There is no reason why we shouldn't share with them, encourage them and actually join with them in walking the aisle with God. Yet, in many cases, we are actually holding back the numbers who are willing to commit themselves fully to the will of God. We are not willing to pay the price ourselves, and to compensate for our own lack of commitment we have either unconcernedly or unwittingly become a stumblingblock in the pathway of those who *are* willing to trust God with every detail of their lives.

There is so much we have yet to learn about dedication. And, unfortunately, some Christians will never come to understand that it is far better to give than to receive, far easier to pay the price than to withhold that which rightfully belongs to God, and far better to hold friends, money, love and possessions in an open palm than to clench one's fist and try to keep for oneself that which was given to be shared with others.

Jesus said, "Anyone who wants to be my follower must love me far more than he does . . . his own life—otherwise he cannot be my disciple. And no one can be my disciple who does not carry his own cross and follow me. But don't begin until you count the cost. For who would begin construction of a building without first getting estimates and then checking to see if he has enough money to pay the bills? Otherwise he might complete only the foundation before running out of funds. And how everyone would laugh! 'See that fellow there?' they would mock. 'He started that building and ran out of money before it was finished!' . . . So no one can become my disciple unless he first sits down and counts his blessings—and then renounces them all for me" (Luke 14:26-30, 33, The Living Bible).

The cost of dedication is great, but the rewards cannot be compared with any worldly gain. Of a truth, "You get what you pay for" . . . and far more!

14

What Problems Does Dedication Raise?

Decisions almost always involve change. And most of us are not too keen on change! The result if change does not occur, of course, is apathy, unconcern and/or stagnation. Simply maintaining the *status quo* is another way of treading water. We work hard and long, but go nowhere, and barely manage to keep our head above water. We slip into a rut, which is nothing more than an open-ended, shallow, uncovered grave.

There are problems connected with change—usually surmountable with a minimum of effort—but are, nevertheless, present.

Dedication is a crossroad's experience. You are moving along in one direction, but are now heading off in another. The old familiar landmarks are no longer a guide. It is a whole new experience. At first it may be difficult to follow the new road signs, especially if some of them have been torn down or were never put up. There may be steep hills and sharp turns which had not been anticipated. You may question why you decided to travel this road. Or others may ask for an explanation of why you chose this path.

Perhaps one of the most difficult problems one has to face concerns those whose parents refuse to permit their son or daughter to follow the pathway of dedication. Unsaved parents can be a stumblingblock to one committed to full-time Christian service. Arguments will be given trying to undermine the credibility and confidence of the young person. More than once it has happened that with no sense of sacrifice, a young person has had to leave home in order to pursue his calling by which God called him. Some have been threatened with being cut out of an inheritance. Some have had their lives threatened. Some have even witnessed a funeral service performed on their behalf to indicate that the parents no longer consider their son or daughter a living part of the family. These things happen in America. They happen with even more regularity in other countries of the world.

If a young child has offered himself in dedication, he is obligated to follow the dictates of his parents, for he is subject to them. In the Word of God, we do not find any special clause attached to the command to honor and obey our parents that would excuse a child from parental guidance, even though those parents may not be saved.

Somehow, we Americans have forgotten that children are children until they come of age. Today's young people are intelligent—far more so than I was at their age. Many of them have been allowed freedom of thought and action such as we have never witnessed before in our 200-year history. Discipline has been noticeably lacking. It's not at all unusual to see a 3- or 4-year-old telling his parents exactly what he will or will

not do, or what he will or will not say. Because
in some ways our children *seem* older and *seem*
smarter, we have disallowed them the privilege
of being children. We forget that they are not wise.
They are not mature. They are not able to cope
adequately with the adult world without a goodly
amount of instruction, training and experience.

The Lord says very clearly in His Word, "Children, obey your parents; this is the right thing
to do because God has placed them in authority
over you. Honor your father and mother. This is
the first of God's Ten Commandments that ends
with a promise. And this is the promise: that if
you honor your father and mother, yours will be
a long life, full of blessing" (Eph. 6:1-3, The Living Bible). Paul wrote again to Christian children
as recorded in Colossians 3:20, "Children, obey
your parents in all things: for this is well pleas-
ing unto the Lord."

Dedication requires discipline and discipline
must begin at home.

When, however, a child becomes of age, he is
legally free to make his own choices in life. And
as a free agent, he has every right to choose Christian service as his life's goal. Then it is that he
can encourage himself with Peter's words as he
stated, "We ought to obey God rather than men"
(Acts 5:29). This doesn't ever mean that he goes
back to his parents to say, "I told you so!" Obedience to God must take precedence in every experience of life. With that obedience there should be
a humility and acknowledgment of the part his
parents have played in his instruction and training.

Even though a child may be held back from

actively pursuing Christian service until he is legally free to do so, we would not minimize the necessity for a child to allow his love and obedience to God to permeate his attitudes and actions. Too many Christian children have been asked to empty the garbage, do the dishes, or walk the dog, only to reply, "I can't do it. I'm on my way to give out tracts," or "I'm dressed for church," or "Let George do it."

On the other hand, when a matter comes up and the requested action is against the moral attributes of God, even a child has every right to take his stand on the side of his Lord. There *are* times when a child must "be about the Father's business," just as the Lord Jesus went into the temple to speak with the learned men of His day. He apparently became so engrossed in asking and answering questions that He completely forgot about His parents. His commitment to the Father was so strong that He was oblivious to all else. Nevertheless, after His parents located Him we are told, "And he went with them, and came to Nazareth, and was subject unto them" (Luke 2:51).

There can also be problems when parents *are* Christians. It is very difficult to watch the little birds fly away from the nest. Many parents protectively smother their children, planning their future so that the least amount of danger, peril and unhappiness result . . . at least to their thinking. A father has waited a whole generation to add the words "and son" to his company name. A mother, thwarted from becoming a nurse because of family circumstances, financial needs or marriage strongly insists upon this career for her daughter. You will even find committed Christians who try by every means to dissuade their children from becoming pastors and missionaries. Unfortunately, much of this is due to lack of adequate teaching within the church itself concerning the opportunities of these professions, and the false, but all too poignant image of missionaries which has been given to the world (i.e., terrible living conditions, unhealthy climates, unfriendly natives, ever-present snakes and other awful creatures, lack of financial remuneration, *ad infinitum* and *ad nauseum*). Few parents have joyfully given up their children without a struggle to face such formidable foes. The image of full-time Christian workers is slowly changing, but not rapidly enough.

So children from Christian homes also face problems with the process of dedication. (How happy God must be with Christian parents who, though they dearly love their children, are willing to turn them over to Christian service in the will of God. Their names will undoubtedly be listed beside the names of Abraham and Hannah in the Lord's book of remembrance.)

For those who are ready for education in order to prepare themselves for full-time Christian service, those who are already in training, and those older folks who have long since completed their education, there are other problems.

When the missionary era of the church re-commenced, men and women went forth with little formal academic training. Most were self-taught or church-taught in the Word of God.

With the beginning of the 20th century, we saw the rise of Bible schools and Bible colleges. Almost all missionaries during the past half century have been required to have formal Bible training in preparation for service overseas and at home. Usually a 3-year Bible course fulfilled the requirements for missionary candidates. In special instances, only one year was demanded, if an academic degree had previously been acquired in the liberal arts, or if a nurse had obtained her R.N. or an engineer had completed his course in a technical school or university. Seminary training, although desirable, was not a standard requirement even for missionary pastors and teachers.

But we are living in a new day. Academic requirements are becoming higher and more rigid around the world. This is due, mainly, to the fact that newly emerging nations are doing far more for themselves than ever before. For example, missionaries provided the first schools in the nation of Nigeria. They did a good job for several scores of years. But now Nigeria has a fine staff of their own teachers, capable of providing much of the education for their own children.

It is interesting to note that at the end of World War II there were only 2 universities in all of tropical Africa. Today there are 23.

Even the standards of the national church in previously underdeveloped countries are becoming higher. This means that nationals being trained for leadership positions must be more highly qualified. These leaders learn fast, and are capable of taking over in many areas (as they have done in many parts of Kenya, Nigeria and Latin America, as well as in other parts of the world).

All of this means that the Christian worker today must be more highly trained than ever before. He is being placed in a position of leadership and training, and being used as a consultant and resource person.

This raises problems for the one who has dedicated his life for full-time Christian service in that it means he must obtain the best possible education. This will cost a lot of money—but the God who calls you to His service is not a pauper! He may have to re-direct his thinking so that rather than going forth as a generalist or an evangelist, he will go out as a skilled worker in communications, mechanics, literature, or in any one of scores of possible majors.

With excellent training, another problem crops up. You are now in a position to obtain a well-paying job in the homeland. Why shouldn't you accept such work so you can give financial help to those who have gone forth to the ends of the earth? A worthy plan! But a problem, too. You told the Lord you'd go into full-time Christian work. You prepared for it and declared over and over again that you felt God wanted you on the mission field. Has the unimportant matter of finances caused you to turn a deaf ear to God's call? Has your dollar-driven energy been captured by a lesser concern? True, God calls some to stay home and provide finances for His work. But did He call *you* to it? Or was this your own idea? Did someone talk you into it? Does it seem like an easier path to tread? Oh, be sure, my friend, before you make a decision based on financial advantage, even if it seems to be profitable to God.

For those who serve their Lord in the homeland, academic requirements are also high. Gone are the days when just anyone could enter the ministry. Even twenty-five years ago, during my Bible school years, students were given barely passing grades even though they were actually failing their subjects. Their sincerity and "dedication" was responsible for some very excellent instructors to "push them through" so they could enter Christian service. The years have matured some of those graduates in their thinking and ministry, but others have never begun to swim in the stream of life. They are standing at the water's edge, just as they did twenty-five years ago when they were handed their diploma.

But there are thousands of Bible school graduates who studied diligently, learned well, and went on to further their education at institutions of higher education, including seminaries and universities. Many now have an earned doctoral degree, although they have long since finished their formal academic training, they are desirous of continuing their learning through workshops, seminars, conferences and other noncredit types of learning experiences, including their own personal study. Christian workers deal with every class, age and educationally prepared individual. It behooves them, therefore, to be fully trained for their work.

There are further problems in the educational aspect of those dedicated to full-time Christian service. Some people do not have the discipline and desire to obtain further education. Some work much better with their hands than with their minds. And something very important must be remembered—education does not guarantee a good Christian worker. There is the matter of meeting the needs of the whole person through Christian service. Not every person is capable of doing this. There is certainly a problem when a psychologically unbalanced individual seeks to assume a place of distinction in Christian work. This is a very difficult thing to handle. Yet it is the responsibility of the church to cope with it in its infancy.

There may come another problem in the plans of a person dedicated to the Lord for missionary service. He may not be able to go to the field which he feels God has "laid upon his heart." In my own case, I had hoped to go to China. But the doors to China closed. I decided that was the end of missions for me. But I had no peace about my decision, even after I was accepted by a Home Mission organization for work in this country. As I waited upon the Lord, it was made very clear— I thought—that I should go to the Muslim people of India. I followed through on this, feeling confident that God would open up the way before me. Yet, three times my visa was refused. Two years had passed, and my dedication was giving me problems! But all of a sudden, West Pakistan threw open its doors and within two months I was among Muslim people who were formerly Indians.

Missionaries can no longer plan too far ahead as to where they are going to serve. And they may not get to a place simply because that is where *they* want to go. Visas are getting more and more difficult to obtain for many countries of the world. More restrictions are being laid down. It is very possible that you will have to be willing to go to a place that wants *you*, rather than to a place where you want to go. We, of course, are guests in the countries where we serve. It is up to each government to decide when and if and who and why they want missionaries. And it is highly possible that they won't want or need *you!*

Many countries feel it is wrong for Americans to be doing the work *they* can do. In some cases we are not prepared for this type of treatment. But we have failed to train national leadership, and they are left to cope as best they can without the counsel of the missionary. In other areas, Christian workers are being allowed entrance only as instructors, supervisors, administrators and/or consultants. With nationals taking over positions formerly held by and duties performed by missionaries, it should mean an increase in the missionary force, for not only are these missionaries released for ministries in other countries or in the homeland, but the national church should be producing its own Christian workers. Should you go to a country where you may be replaced by a national within a short time? Is this a waste?

Some countries are now limiting the number of visas they will issue to any one agency serving within their borders. Other countries have not yet restricted the number of visas to a definite quota, but if Americans continue to flood in, they may decide to do so. The United States, of course, has a policy restricting the immigration of people from certain countries of the world, so it is not surprising that other governments are proceeding in the same way. The problem is, if only a certain number of visas are to be given, will your work be of enough value to allow you the privilege of receiving one of them? And if your visa is refused, where do you go from there?

Work at home provides problems for the one who is dedicated to full-time Christian service, too.

There are innumerable positions open. You can be a Bible school professor, a house parent, a secretary or bookkeeper in a Christian office, a youth director, youth pastor, child or youth evangelism worker, college campus worker, teacher or administrator in a Christian school, a worker in the home office of a mission society, a Rescue Mission director or worker, musician, Christian education director, church secretary, chalk artist, evangelist, coffee-house director, ghetto worker, Christian psychologist, editor, author, home missionary, etc. You can work in the city, the suburbs, a rural area, within an ethnic group, on street corners, in colleges, in churches, in homes, in schools, in institutions, alone or with co-workers. There are so many different opportunities, so many neglected people, so many needy areas. Where does one begin? How does one know God's will? Should one work independently? If not, how does one choose an organization under which he can serve? Dedication always brings up the problem of choosing the best from a multitude of "good" things.

Waiting for a "call" from God can be a problem, especially to one who may not know of what a "call" consists. Many dedicated workers stand at the crossroads far too long, waiting for a definite call and a full knowledge of the will of God. This waiting has resulted in thousands missing out on *any* opportunity for Christian service. Not being able to distinguish the "call," they have given themselves to tasks which did not result in full-time Christian service.

In her book, *Through Gates of Splendor*, Elisabeth Elliot quotes Pete Fleming as writing, "A

call is nothing more nor less than obedience to
the will of God, as God presses it home to the
soul by whatever means He chooses." [1]

God calls individuals. I cannot say what the
call of God is for *your* life, nor can you tell what
His call is for *mine*. But *you* will know it as you
give yourself to Him and wait upon Him in prayer
and patience. Just as we find God by truly seeking,
so we find His call by seeking it.

As far as having a *full* knowledge of the will
of God, we cannot hope to receive this at a designated moment. He reveals His will one step at
a time. Some visionaries have planned their entire
lifetime and feel they *do* know God's will for their
lives. This is very good, but life is filled with var-
iables, and often that which we had planned cannot, in the will of God, come to pass. Discover-
ing God's will is a daily reliance upon Him. James
was a practical Christian. He says, "Go to now,
ye that say, Today or tomorrow we will go into
such a city and continue there a year, and buy
and sell, and get gain: whereas ye know not what
shall be on the morrow. For what is your life?
It is even a vapour, that appeareth for a little
time, and then vanisheth away. For that ye ought
to say, If the Lord will, we shall live, and do
this, or that" (James 4:13-15). This doesn't mean
we shouldn't dream dreams and make plans. It
simply implies that we really do not have a full
knowledge of the will of God from the cradle to

---

1. *Through Gates of Splendor* by Elisabeth Elliot, Spire Pub-
lications, Fleming H. Revell Co., Old Tappan, New Jersey (1970,
p. 22).

the grave. A sudden turn of events can produce problems in the life of one who has dedicated himself to full-time Christian service.

Another large problem concerning the dedicated individual comes when a husband or wife does not have the same desire to enter full-time Christian service that the mate does. This has kept thousands of individuals from marrying one whom they had planned to marry. It has brought strife to Christian homes. It has brought about divorce. It has resulted in a good many entering full-time Christian service who were not willing for it, and this, in turn, has resulted in severe psychological, physical and emotional problems, for one cannot live indefinitely under such stress without reaching a breaking point.

This problem can also produce difficult situations for others. While I was a worker at the home office of a mission board, the director received a letter from a man who wrote something like this: "I long to serve God. I feel called to the mission field. My wife doesn't have the same desire, but I want to go anyway. By the way, what is your pay scale?"

Another time a dear lady showed up in the office having traveled some 5,000 miles to get there. In conversation she told the director, "My husband doesn't feel called, but I'm going anyway." After several conferences, the board refused to allow this woman to go out under their auspices. But she went out independently, ignoring all advice.

In each of these cases, it was not the Lord but their unhappy marriages that "called" them to Christian service. Discerning God's will and our own will in matters concerning Christian service can be a difficult problem. Others may give counsel, but only God has the answers for all concerned.

There are, indeed, many problems which those who dedicate themselves to full-time Christian service may have to face. What about a divorced person? What about one who has served a prison sentence? What about one who was a juvenile delinquent? What about those who are of less than normal intelligence? What of those who can't manage to get along with other people? What of those with severe physical handicaps? Even those who seem to be completely qualified for service may encounter problems because of a lack of concern by their family, church, or the organization under which they choose to serve.

Life is filled with problems of one kind or another. Just because one has dedicated himself for full-time Christian service does not in any way automatically eliminate his everyday problems. In some matters they may even seem insurmountable. But he has the God of the impossible on his side. As he leans heavily upon the wisdom God gives and follows the leading of the Holy Spirit, the way will be made clear before him. If an individual truly gives himself to the Lord in love and obedience for Him, and for that reason alone, God will honor him for it. "Yea, I have spoken it, I will also bring it to pass; I have purposed it, I will also do it" (Isa. 46:11). "Faithful is he that calleth you, who also will do it" (1 Thess. 5:24).

15

The "S" Sense of Dedication

Every Christian organization has a verse of Scripture upon which it seeks to base its operations. This is true of the mission board under which I served in Pakistan.

When I first heard of the board, I was told of its foundation verse. Later, whenever I saw an advertisement sponsored by them, the verse appeared. Their letterhead contained a portion of the verse. And in spite of all this, I never consciously considered what those words meant.

It is now twenty years since I set sail for missionary service. God has been steadily at work during this time, and although I have failed Him many times over, He has guided and led, and, I believe, kept me true to that hour in which I walked down an aisle and dedicated my life to full-time Christian service. I do not serve in the way I had hoped, for my missionary service overseas was cut short by sickness. But through the years, I have come to understand that full-time service does not necessarily equate with *missionary* service. And I believe I am, at last, beginning to understand some of the implications of the verse of Scripture to which I once paid little or no attention.

What is the verse? It is found in Isaiah 54:2, "Enlarge the place of thy tent, and let them stretch forth the curtains of thine habitations: spare not, lengthen thy cords, and strengthen thy stakes."

I'm sure you, too, have read or heard these words many times in regard to the extension of the kingdom and the preaching of the gospel. But we have in this verse the very essence of dedication to full-time service. I call it the "S" sense because it is found in three words or phrases beginning with the letter "S"—namely: (1) stretch forth; (2) spare not; and (3) strengthen thy stakes.

There was a time when only Boy Scouts and inveterate fishermen set up tents in the wilderness. Those days belong to the distant past. We are now living in a day when camping seems to hold a very high place in the hearts of many Americans. And because camping is so prevalent, most of us know something about it.

Of course, many so-called campers take an easier route to "tenting out." With mobile campers of every size, shape and description, it is fairly easy to set up camp. With some of the "tag-along-behind" equipment, all you have to do is press certain buttons upon arrival at the campsite and lo, an instant tent!

But these are not the truly back-to-nature campers. Their equipment serves them well, is practical and up-to-date. But for sheer thrills, there is nothing like putting up your own canvas tent and sleeping on the ground or on a rickety cot.

If one is to sleep in a tent, he wants to be sure no wind, rain or animal is going to disturb his rest. How many outdoorsmen have had a tent collapse, or blown away? Or perhaps they have awakened to see a bear eating the chocolate bars from their knapsacks? And the less experienced the camper, the more likely it will be that such calamities will befall him! This is another area of life where we live and learn!

But what does all of this have to do with dedication to full-time Christian service? Let's consider that question.

Stretch Forth

The very fact of walking down the aisle is confirmation of a heart's desire to "enlarge the place of thy tent." It is all too easy to stay in a corner, do a good job, but let the world pass by. True, there may be far fewer problems and responsibilities if one doesn't stick out his neck, but it is also true that you must climb out on a limb if you want to pick the fruit. It seldom grows on the solid trunk of the tree! Reaching out to others should be a normal characteristic of the Christian life. A tent does little good toward the purpose for which it was created if it is not "stretched out." All of us need to be stretched out if we are to be usable and useful.

How do we need to stretch? There is no doubt about it. We must stretch in every direction. Our mentality needs to be trained and sharpened. Our emotions must be controlled and temperate. Our self-image must be brought into clear focus. Our inter-personal relationships must be improved and broadened. Our theology must become what we are, and not what we say. Our talents, skills and abilities must be brought into a place of accountability. Physically, we should maintain a program of the best health habits.

Within the body of Christ, those who are dedicated to full-time Christian service must be assisted by others who are willing to help them in stretching. Opportunities for service must be opened to them. Financial recources must also be made available.

If a man doesn't know how to set up a tent, he will do best to find someone who *does* know how. Then he must watch carefully, observe closely, follow instructions, learn some of the facts of which he was previously unaware, and finally, do the work to the best of his ability. He cannot always watch. He cannot always listen to instructions. He must, sooner or later, come to a point in time when he actually puts all of this into practice. His tent will stay put or fall down according to the expertise of his teacher and his own ability to do what he has set out to accomplish.

It is simple enough to attend services in a church setting. Everything goes along quite smoothly and outwardly there is little indication of all that is involved in Christian service. Things just seem to happen at the right time and in the right way. This, of course, is not the true picture. It is much like an outfielder who makes an impossible catch of a fly ball. The television screen makes it appear as though it were a very normal occurrence, involving a minimum of effort and know-how. Little thought is given to the one who accomplished the slight miracle. No one remembers those drill sessions, the hours of running, the hours of chasing balls, the days of being coached. It's just another fly ball that was caught—a source of joy to some and a reason for sadness to others.

Christian service does not come naturally. It is only the stretching, flexing and strengthening of spiritual muscles that makes the impossible happen. Unfortunately, too many give up in the days of training, and they are not, therefore, adequately prepared for the difficult plays of life. These individuals, if they remain in Christian service, become frustrated, disappointed, embittered and fruitless.

Some who hope to enter Christian service forget to do their spiritual exercises—prayer, Bible study, Christian fellowship, service for God. Unused muscles become weak and useless. Medical science proves this conclusively. If you've ever broken an arm or leg, you know exactly how difficult it is to work the appendage after the cast is removed! Our spiritual tone must be kept at its highest pitch at all times. This demands a good deal of exercise.

Those who would enter Christian service are expected to extend themselves to others. But the word "stretch" also has the meaning of "reaching out." The church has always had the idea that this stretching out had to do with reaching those "out there"—wherever "out there" is! Before these dedicated folks can reach out to others, however, they must be given the opportunity of reaching out to the church. Oh yes, God provides and God empowers for service. But the church ought to be involved in the act of stretching forth. If thirty individuals have dedicated their lives to full-time Christian service, they have every reason in the world to reach out to the church for help. Going forth with empty hands to feed a starving world is not the best use of personnel! Churches, we must remember, are capable of becoming soft on sin and weak in effectiveness because of lack of spiritual exercise. They, too, must stretch forth, in an effort to help those who are dedicated.

It costs something to stretch forth. Sometimes it is painful. Sometimes the body resists it. It usually disperses close-knit cliques. It produces pressures. Apathetic individuals will not participate. Those who are unconcerned for the health of the total body will refuse to become involved. But it is an essential part of dedication.

Spare Not

Christian service takes time, money, talents, people. Can a church afford to lose a deacon, an elder, a Sunday school teacher, a youth leader? Can it and will it gladly allow those recent retirees to use their finances to support themselves in Christian work rather than continuing to give those funds to the church treasury?

How often has it been the church which has limited the zeal of those who are willing to be Christian workers? How many times have willing witnesses been hindered because of a fear of injury, harm or evil which might befall them in His service? The fear of lack of finances, the fear of illness, a fear of dealing head-on with the powers of darkness! For those willing to go overseas the church has said, "But the road is too hard and dangerous. Have you considered work in the homeland? After all, charity begins at home." And for those who determine to work at home comes the unnerving question from the church, "Have you considered overseas work?" Although not always done with the best intentions, it is, indeed, the responsibility of the church to tell both sides of the story. Then it is up to the individual to choose, in the will of God, that for which he feels most qualified. And the church ought to allow each individual to discover God's will and pursue it without hindrance.

Christian workers should not be given up as a part of the church which is not strictly needed. These ought not to be surplus stock. They should be the cream of the crop.

The church should not be frugal or live in a savingly stinting manner. God cannot use that which is held in a tightly closed fist. The church has a responsibility to give freely of its people to the service of Christ. God has a way of multiplying by dividing. Giving the best of your membership to full-time Christian service is one way to cause a church to show immeasurable growth and maturity.

God's word says, "Spare not." What is a spare room, a spare part, or a spare tire? Isn't it something which is not being used? Something which is being held for future and/or emergency use? Isn't it something not presently needed? God is reminding the church that we ought not to grasp onto every member to fill the immediate ranks of the church, and to count on for future vacancies. "Give and it shall be given unto you," the Lord assured us. May no pastor or congregation be found guilty of holding back Christian workers from their dedication by the old excuse, "What will we ever do without you?" Nor should any man be egotistical enough to believe that he is, indeed, indispensable!

And you who are dedicated must also heed.

God says, "Spare not." Don't hold anything back from Him. Don't just give Him the leftovers. Give Him your first and your best. Spare no time, spare no expense, spare no effort in getting the gospel of Christ to the ends of the earth.

God gave us an example of His injunction to "spare not," not through a parable, but through His own fulfillment of that command. We are told by Peter (2 Pet. 2:4) that God spared not the angels; Romans 11:21 tells us that God spared not His own people, Israel; and Romans 8:32 declares that He spared not His own Son.

God never asks us to do anything He himself is not willing to do. We have adequate confirmation in Scripture that He spared not. And His desire for us is that we "spare not."

Strengthen Thy Stakes

The further a tent is stretched forth, the deeper its stakes must be driven. Otherwise the tent will not long endure! It is quite obvious that short ropes are for small tents. As the tent enlarges, longer ropes must be utilized. But what about the stakes? It takes a bit of effort to find long, strong stakes and those who are willing to put labor into hammering those stakes deeply into the ground.

It has been said that a chain is no stronger than its weakest link. It is also true that without a strong home base, the soldier in the field is defenseless. And if a government cannot back up its currency, that currency is of no value. Unless a manufacturer will guarantee his product and give help when it is necessary, the product has little usefulness.

What is the responsibility of the church to those

who dedicate themselves to full-time service? Surely it is to become a strong link in the chain. It is to strengthen the stakes at the home base. It is to back up its Christian workers in every way possible. It is to stand behind the ones it sends forth, guaranteeing that their testimony is pure and undefiled, and promising to repair any defects which may be found along the way. This is not a once-in-a-lifetime task. It is a continual challenge, for there should be a constant enlarging of the tent by means of those who dedicate themselves to the Lord for His service.

By strengthening the stakes, we do not necessarily mean that the home church must physically enlarge, or that it must build a multi-million dollar complex, or that it must hire several assistant pastors and other workers. There are occasions when the church does enlarge. There are right times to build larger and more adequate facilities. As the congregation increases in size, more paid workers must be engaged. But we are here speaking of strengthening the spiritual core of the local church. As men and women, boys and girls dedicate themselves to giving, to praying, to witnessing, to teaching, and to helping in whatever way possible, the stakes will be strengthened. Those who go forth in Christian service will be upheld by the strengthening and sustaining power of those spiritual stakes.

And what about the individuals who would serve full time? They, too, must strengthen their own stakes. They must seek to improve their effectiveness through adequate training. They must become stronger in their reliance upon God. They must be reinforced against the forces of the world, the flesh and the devil.

Webster tells us that "to strengthen" applies to any increasing of force, vigor, power, intensity or effectiveness. Jesus told Peter, "Strengthen thy brethren" (Luke 22:32). There is not only the need for the church to strengthen the brethren, but there is the very real sense in which the brethren must, in turn, strengthen the church. As the tent is enlarged, there is, on the part of both the church and those dedicated to full-time Christian service, the Lord's admonition to "stretch forth . . . spare not . . . and strengthen thy stakes."

This, then, is the "S" sense of dedication. Has it been *your* experience? Are you willing for it to be? If so, you will seek more than ever to direct people to that aisle walk with God, you will experience the blessing of God upon your ministry, and this book will not have been written in vain.

OTHER BOOKS
YOU MAY WANT TO READ

MANUAL FOR FOLLOWERS OF JESUS
by William (Winkey) Pratney

A total guidebook for Christian life and service. Clearly laid out under headings like "The Disciple's Salvation," "The Disciple's Spiritual Life," "The Disciple's Stand," "The Disciple's Self-control," etc. The famous youth writer and speaker touches on all the subjects which are likely to be problem areas, like evolution, sex, temptation, music, and self-control. $3.50

THE NEW SOVEREIGNTY
by Reginald Wallis

Wallis asserts there is no remission apart from submission, and no alliance without allegiance. A challenging call to New Testament discipleship. $1.25

TEN STEPS TO THE GOOD LIFE (originally published under the title THE LAW IS HOLY)

by Harold J. Brokke

This is a book about a subject rarely treated by modern authors—the Ten Commandments. It is a very positive book, showing the relationship of God's laws to happy, successful living. Formerly titled, THE LAW IS HOLY, the book has been revised and is now presented with a striking new cover in our Dimension Books series. $1.50

Purchase these books at your local bookstore. If your bookstore does not have them, you may order from Bethany Fellowship, Inc., 6820 Auto Club Road, Minneapolis, Minnesota 55438. Enclose payment with your order, plus 10¢ per book for postage.